UNIVERSITY
GOALS
AND
ACADEMIC
POWER

EDWARD GROSS *68-59086*
PAUL V. GRAMBSCH

AMERICAN COUNCIL ON EDUCATION
WASHINGTON, D.C.

COMMISSION ON
ADMINISTRATIVE AFFAIRS
Appointed by the American Council on Education

FOREWORD

Almost everywhere these days there is a lively debate about the means and ends of American higher education. On many campuses, it proceeds in orderly ways, but on others, it spills over into dissension and strife. Almost nowhere, however, has there been a systematic effort to get at the precise nature and scope of differing views about the perceived and preferred roles of various members of the academic community.

This study by Edward Gross and Paul V. Grambsch on UNIVERSITY GOALS AND ACADEMIC POWER is therefore a very timely contribution to needed knowledge. Unlike most other writings on the subject, it is not simply an expression of the authors' opinions and penchants. Instead, it brings together in one volume the observations and attitudes of thousands of academicians on dozens of university campuses throughout the nation. Impressive arrays of data are used to substantiate generalizations and conclusions that have a very direct bearing on all the current talk about what universities are and what they ought to be.

In a period of dynamic change, this volume is recommended reading for all who want a better understanding of some fundamental issues that are agitating the inhabitants of academe. Its empirical approach brings underlying problems into much sharper focus than has hitherto been the case, and supplies a factual basis for considering modifications of structure and functions. The findings of UNIVERSITY GOALS AND ACADEMIC POWER can, in my opinion, help replace heat with light to guide our forward movement out of the confusions regarding the present and future of many institutions of higher learning.

Logan Wilson, President
American Council on Education

iii

PREFACE

Although all major segments of the academic community are concerned with the goals and objectives of their own institutions, college and university presidents and their administrative staffs have a special responsibility, as a vital aspect of their leadership function, to develop, organize, and use the resources of the institution to achieve its goals with maximum effectiveness. An essential phase of this goal-oriented function is to clarify the institution's present goals, and especially to distinguish between the real and the supposed, in order to evaluate the effectiveness of progress toward these goals—and, equally important, continually to reevaluate the goals themselves. As needs and contexts change, so may goals.

The original report upon which this volume is based appeared in a form and under circumstances which would probably never have brought it to the attention of most academic administrators.[1] It was submitted as a multigraphed document to the Office of Education, Department of Health, Education, and Welfare, in June 1967, and was therefore not widely available. In the second place, its length and the wealth of technical detail make it too forbidding for most busy administrators—and especially for those whose favorite reading material does *not* include scholarly and statistical reports.

Yet those of us who had the good fortune to come upon it and the patience to scale the massive but unavoidable walls of facts and numbers found stimulating ideas and materials which we felt should be summarized and brought to the attention of a broad audience of academic leaders in all kinds of institutions—not merely those in the small population of universities studied by the authors.

The Commission on Administrative Affairs is sponsoring publication of a much-abridged version, substantially rewritten by Laura Kent, designed expressly for the busy administrator who

---

[1] *Academic Administrators and University Goals*. (Final Report, Project Bureau No. 5078 (formerly project 2633), Contract No. SAE OE 5-10-099. June 1967. U.S. Department of Health, Education, and Welfare, Office of Education, Bureau of Research.)

v

might have neither the time nor the opportunity to read the original and who is not as interested in the theoretical roots and technical details of the study as he is in its potentially significant contents. (Those who may wish to challenge some of the occasionally startling conclusions or who wish to understand in greater detail how they were reached can turn to the original report.)

UNIVERSITY GOALS AND ACADEMIC POWER should be of widespread interest, especially to academic administrators and faculty leaders, for several reasons.

First, it is one of the few objective studies ever undertaken, at least on such an ambitious scale, of the actual goals of universities, as perceived by administrators and faculty members, and of the differences between these perceptions and the preferences of those responsible for goal definition and achievement.

Second, some of the conclusions reached by Professor Gross and Dean Grambsch run counter to much academic folklore and should provoke some lively discussion and fresh thought about the goals of higher education in America.

Third, the methodology itself suggests that it is misleading at best and dangerous at worst to take anything for granted about either the real or the apparent goals of institutions or of the individuals who both influence these goals and presumably strive to achieve them. The simplest benefit which might follow a study of this volume would be an attempt on the part of academic leaders, in colleges as well as universities, to answer such questions as the following about their own institutions.

: What are our actual goals at the present time?
: Are we sure we distinguish clearly between our output goals and our support goals?
: What if any dissonances exist between our statements about our goals and our actual goals as revealed by what we are in fact doing?
: Again, what if any dissonances exist between our real or presumed goals and the goals which leading members or leaders of our institution really prefer?
: How are our goals really determined—and by whom?

As is often true in self-study activities, the questions asked may turn out to be more valuable than the answers and the process of self-examination more constructive than the formal results.

One may argue endlessly about the locus of "real" responsibility for setting an institution's goals, and the means of achieving them and of defining the support goals necessary for their achievement may differ from one institution to another. But it is certainly one of the functions of leadership, be it by administrator, faculty, trustee, or whomever, continually to clarify these goals and periodically to re-examine them in the light of changing desirabilities and feasibilities.

One may also argue at length about whether the 47 goals studied by the authors include all those which might be appropriate for every institution—or about whether the stated goals are too detailed or too concise. However, they make a telling point by the very breadth of coverage attempted. Most discussions about goals are extremely limited and very general in scope, and hence it is often difficult to evaluate the effectiveness or completeness of their achievement. Gross and Grambsch have performed a valuable service in illustrating the depth and breadth of detail with which it is possible to define and evaluate the goals of a complex institution. Whatever one thinks of their particular list of 47 goals, it provides a model and a starting point, a straw man which one may tear apart, reconstruct, and add to or subtract from at will. But, to stretch the analogy, the straw man also exhibits a commendable level of *detailed modeling*.

So much for methods and techniques of analysis and for sharpness of focus. As to content, both administrators and faculty will find some surprises, not all of them pleasant and many of them surely controversial. At this point I will not steal the authors' thunder and will refer the reader to the summary in Chapter 6. Among the conclusions which interested me were that administrators and faculty are in some respects closer and farther apart in their views than either seems to think at times—and that some of the criticisms leveled at higher education by students and by faculty reformers, whether they are "correct" or not, reflect real differences in goals rather than in views about the means to achieve them.

As the authors of this volume point out, means can sometimes appear to be—or to become—goals in themselves. Much time might be saved, and some frustrations reduced, by distinguishing between real and presumed or apparent differences of opinion about goals. This study's findings seem to suggest that there are more agreements than may commonly be supposed, and thus it may be helpful to concentrate on the remainder, the real disagreements, as well as to strive continually to bring presently perceived and actually preferred goals into harmony.

NOTE.—The *very* busy reader may wish to glance very briefly at the technical and theoretical materials in Chapter 1 and then go on to Chapters 2 *et seq.*, and to the results of the study. If these intrigue or startle him sufficiently, he may then find Chapter 1 more relevant or helpful. (At any rate, *this* particular reader found himself inclined to skip the background material until a foundation for being concerned about technology had been laid by the curiosity and amazement aroused by some of the substantive findings.)

The academic world has changed a little since 1964, the year in which the data were gathered for this study. However, most of the findings still seem to ring true in 1968—and, indeed, some of them may explain some of the changes which have taken place or which are being advocated. No matter how different circumstances may be after four years, Professor Gross and Dean Grambsch provide a useful framework for an objective, stimulating, and constructive approach which the leadership of any academic institution might find it profitable to consider.

John Caffrey, Director
Commission on Administrative Affairs

Washington, D.C., August 14, 1968

CONTENTS

LIST OF TABLES

INTRODUCTION

This volume presents the results of an analysis of the roles of university administrators and the organization of American universities. It is intended to provide an overview of the approach used and the method employed together with some of the major findings on the goals of universities. It is also designed for those who so kindly filled out our lengthy questionnaire, the administrators themselves. We have therefore striven for readability and for limited technical footnotes and references and have deliberately limited such discussion to an Appendix.

We plan to prepare other books based on the data we collected in this investigation. Our other studies will deal with the careers of administrators and with the decision-making process in universities. In still other studies we expect to focus on role-conceptions of administrators and on structures of authority in universities. These studies will not necessarily be issued by the American Council on Education.

To Laura Kent we owe a great debt of gratitude for thorough editorial work and extensive rewriting of this book. Miss Kent was particularly skillful in clarifying points we thought too technical or abstruse. Often she was able to show us that such points were only abstruse to us. We are grateful for the publishing sponsorship of the Commission on Administrative Affairs, American Council on Education, and for the time spent by the Commission's Director, John Caffrey, in additional editorial work and assistance in organization of the material for the nontechnical reader. Finally, to Council President Logan Wilson we owe a special debt for encouraging us to organize this material in its present form and for drawing upon the resources of the Council to make this publication possible.

Edward Gross
Professor of Sociology
University of Washington

Paul V. Grambsch
Dean, School of Business Administration
Summer 1968   University of Minnesota

CHAPTER 1

UNIVERSITY GOALS: AN OVERVIEW

In many organizations, becoming an administrator is regarded as evidence of upward mobility. Such seems to be the case in businesses, factories, the armed services, and most government agencies. When an organization begins to employ large numbers of professional persons, however, particularly of scientists who are committed to the values of original research, the status of the administrator often changes. In hospitals, research laboratories, and universities, occupancy of an administrative post may inspire mixed feelings. In a large business, a man's elevation to department head is greeted with congratulations by his friends and colleagues. In a university, on the other hand, a man's accepting a position as a chairman or as dean may be the occasion for expressions of condolence. Not infrequently, the person who assumes such a position will himself derogate it by insisting that it is only temporary or that it was taken on as a duty. Overtly, at least, the feeling is that the fundamental task is the professional or the scientific one and that administration exists largely to facilitate that task. Thus, in the field of nursing, contact with the patient is usually regarded as the significant activity and nursing administration is held to be secondary and to consist of little more than red tape and other bureaucratic activities to be gotten through as soon as possible.

Activities connected with teaching and research are assumed to be the chief reasons why universities exist, though just what these activities are is often not specified. Further, carrying out these tasks is held to be the primary responsibility of the academic staff: that is, of professors, researchers, and their helpers. The administration, it is assumed, has as its main task the providing of support for the academic activities. *Support* is usually defined to include maintenance activities (securing funds and facilities, arranging for counseling, assigning students to classes and dormitories, arranging details of faculty selection and promotion) and integration activities (coordinating departments and schools, settling internal disputes, representing the department or

1

school to outside bodies). Few people would dispute the claim that support activities are necessary, but they are regarded as less important than academic activities.

This situation has, however, been changing during recent years, as academic administration has grown in importance because of certain vast societal changes. The increased professionalization of occupations and the expansion of demand for educated persons sends ever-larger proportions of an expanding population into the universities. International competition produces pressures upon the university to train more scientists and engineers. The accelerated arms and space race leads to a deep penetration of the university by research foundations and government agencies, thus upsetting traditional status relations and forcing many departments or parts of departments into becoming "productive organizations" for paying clients. Such changes are accompanied by major administrative changes in response to demands by state legislatures, private foundations, and governmental agencies for an accounting of how monies are being spent and of whether the organization is being administered in an efficient manner. A major result of this trend has been an increase in the number of administrative personnel (especially in central administration) and in their power.

The size of these increases is not known with any precision, but whatever their dimensions, they have been lamented by many, particularly the academic staff. A growth in the power of administrators represents an upset in the presumed balance between academic activities and support activities on campus. The faculty often grumbles that administrators are overpaid and that too much attention is given to support activities (often called simply red tape) rather than to the goals of the university. Faculty members resent too what they feel to be the illegitimate pretensions of some administrators to "represent" the faculty or the university. The growth in the power of administrators is not, in itself, regarded as necessarily undesirable, even by the academic person (who typically holds highly traditional views of what the university ought to be doing), provided that administrators use their power to help the university attain goals that academic people accept. The situation becomes a source of genuine concern only when administrators are seen both as having more power than the faculty and as using that power to pursue goals considered undesirable or, at least, tangential to desirable goals.

It is clear that in order to answer the question of whether academic administrators constitute a legitimate object of grievance, we need some hard data, such data often being absent from the frequently sterile debates on this issue. In particular, if we are to assess the role of university administrators in the attainment of academic goals, we need to know what the goals of American universities are. This knowledge is often simply taken for granted; rarely is it discussed in any detail, and such statements of goals as are made are usually brief and vague. To say merely that teaching and research are the goals is hardly enough, since it leaves open the central questions: Teaching what, doing research on what, to what extent, and for how long?

This quest for data on the actual goals of universities does not mean that we have no interest in people's conceptions of what the goals ought to be. Quite the contrary: Complaints that any group, administrators or others, is perverting the university's goals should be examined in relation not only to what the goals are, but also to what persons think the goals should be. Hence we must examine the *preferred* as well as the actual goals of those in the academic world.

Those persons concerned with changing goals—whether by halting trends in undesirable directions or by initiating changes in desirable directions—also need information about what factors affect goals. Consequently, in this study we will examine some of the relations between a university's goals and its "global" characteristics—so called because they typify the institution as a whole. The power structure of the university—that is, the relative influence of various persons and groups in making major decisions—will also be examined: first, to determine the extent of the administrat(s power; and second, to explore the relationship between power structure and goals.

The university is a large, complex organization, and consequently, it has a large number of goals. This fact is particularly true of the American university, which has traditionally been under pressure from the local geographical area for practical results and, more recently, from the government for applied research results. Moreover, the university engages in a great many activities without thinking of them as goals. Indeed, if this study has any attributes of originality, they center mainly about the way in which university goals are analyzed and treated. Most persons think of a goal only in terms of some kind of output—teaching, research, and direct service to the community, in the case of the university—but it is our belief that the analysis of university goals requires that many activities normally thought of as maintenance activities be regarded as goals. Our basic premise is that, contrary to the common belief that the university has grown haphazardly, the university is an organization with organizational goals, including maintenance activities. Since so much attention is given to this claim, some theoretical discussion of the concept of organizational goals is necessary.

THE CONCEPT OF ORGANIZATIONAL GOALS

"Goal" is a central concept in the study of organizations. Goal attainment is an aspect of all systems which, in order to survive, must attain whatever goals they set for themselves.[1] In a special kind of system, the formal organization, the problem of goal attainment has primacy over all other problems.[2] In a communal relationship,[3] persons are met for the pleasure intrinsic to the relationship itself, as in the case of a group of friends, a clique, a gang, or a family. Such a group may indeed develop goals (e.g., attacking another group, having a baby), but it does not disband if it fails to attain those goals. It breaks up only when hostilities and cleavages mean that persons are no longer at ease with one another. On the other hand, in an associational relationship, persons are met in order to pursue some goal, and their meeting is a means toward that end. They need not like one another or indeed have feelings any more positive than what is minimally necessary for them to work together to attain the common goals. It is the presence of such goals and the consequent organization of effort to attain them which characterize modern organizations and lead to such accomplishments as healing the sick, attacking an enemy, producing a high standard of living, incarcerating the criminal, organizing the distribution of goods, or administering the affairs of an empire.

[1] See Talcott Parsons *et al.*, (eds.), *Theories of Society* (New York: Free Press of Glencoe, 1961), pp. 38–41.

[2] Talcott Parsons, "A Sociological Approach to the Theory of Formal Organizations," *Structure and Process in Modern Societies* (New York: Free Press of Glencoe, 1960), Ch. 1.

[3] For the distinction between communal and associational relationships, see Robert MacIver, *Community: A Sociological Study* (New York: Macmillan, 1936).

In spite of the great amount of theory and research about formal organizations, surprisingly little attention has been given to defining clearly what is meant by a "goal" in the first place.[4] One scholar defines an organizational goal as "a desired state of affairs which the organization attempts to realize," [5] but this formulation immediately raises the question of *whose* state of affairs it is that is desired. Theoretically, there could be as many desired states for the organization as there are persons in it.

Before one can meaningfully discuss different perceptions of organizational goals, it is essential to distinguish personal from organizational goals. A personal goal is a future state that an individual desires for himself—a definition akin to the psychological concept of motive. This meaning may be distinguished from what a particular person desires *for* the organization as a whole,[6] which may or may not correspond to the organization's group goals. Further, the question arises of how one is to determine an organization's goals when there are differences of opinion among its members. In a small organization, this may not be difficult: The top man's goals for the organization are probably the organization's goals.

But as an organization grows large, many persons may influence its goals.[7] In the case of ideological organizations, where essential personal values presumably coincide, the individual's goals for the organization may correspond closely with the group's goals. Yet one cannot safely make this assumption with most organizations. In fact, it is safer to say that in the typical case these goals will not coincide. Consequently, it is necessary to offer each person an inducement to participate, so that he may attain his personal goal through the group goal of the organization.[8] He must be motivated to the extent that he will give up any dissonant goals of his own for the organization as a whole. Nevertheless, in order to avoid any reification of the concept, it must be emphasized that variant goals will always exist in the

[4] Herbert Simon, "On the Concept of Organization Goal," *Administrative Science Quarterly*, June 1964, 1–22.

[5] Amitai Etzioni, *Modern Organizations* (Englewood Cliffs, N.J.: Prentice-Hall, 1964), p. 6.

[6] See Dorwin Cartwright and Alvin Zander (eds.), *Group Dynamics* (Evanston, Ill.: Row Peterson, 1953), pp. 308–11.

[7] See Richard Cyert and James G. March, *A Behavioral Theory of the Firm* (Englewood Cliffs, N.J.: Prentice-Hall, 1963), Ch. 3.

[8] James G. March and Herbert Simon, *Organizations* (New York: John Wiley and Sons, 1958), Ch. 4.

minds of certain persons. That is to say, although an organizational goal is not necessarily the same thing as a personal goal or as a goal that a particular person desires for an organization, the nature of organizational goals is evident to some extent in the assertions of its members about what they think the organization's goals are.

Some authorities have attempted to define goals in terms of system linkages.[9] They see a goal as involving some type of output to a larger society. In this sense, organizations are always subsystems, the goal of one subsystem being a means or input to another. To take a simple example, the production of carburetors is a goal to the firm that manufactures them but a means or input to an automobile manufacturer. Such an approach emphasizes the relation of organizations to one another and to the surrounding society. Further, when goals are defined in this manner, it becomes clear that those within organizations have limited freedom in setting its goals; they are constrained by what outsiders need or can be persuaded to accept. On the other hand, such an emphasis tends to underestimate the contribution of rational decision-makers in choosing goals; they are not entirely limited by the demands of the market.[10] A more serious drawback to this approach follows from the fact that organizations have a great many outputs, both intended and unintended, many of which will be no different from functions or consequences. It is hard to single out certain kinds of outputs as *the* goals of the organization. The importance of many by-products of industrial processes is also relevant.

All the concepts discussed so far touch on the elements of a definition of goals: Goals exist in someone's mind, and they involve the relationship between an organization and its situation.

The Bureaucratic Personality: A Fruitful Lead

A basic factor in this analysis is the tendency of some persons in some organizations to turn means into ends,[11] a tendency which

9 James D. Thompson and William J. McEwan, "Organization Goals and Environment," *American Sociological Review*, February 1958, 23–31; Parsons, "A Sociological Approach to the Theory of Formal Organizations," p. 17.

10 Cf. the distinction between what Alvin W. Gouldner calls a "rational" and a "natural system" model. "Organizational Analysis," in *Sociology Today*, ed. Robert K. Merton *et al.* (New York: Basic Books, 1959), Ch. 18.

11 Robert K. Merton, "Bureaucratic Structure and Personality," *Social Theory and Social Structure* (Glencoe, Ill.: Free Press, 1957), pp. 195–206. The opening statement in the article reads: "A formal, rationally organized social structure involves clearly defined patterns of activity in which, ideally, every series of actions is functionally related to the purposes of the organization" (p. 95).

has important and often unrecognized implications for the understanding of organizational goals. If an organization is to accomplish its goals, the members must be required to conform to explicit rules. Only through this means can the organization's special advantages of precision, division of labor, and predictability be enjoyed. Yet the very insistence on compliance with rules may lead to a person's forgetting that rules exist, after all, only to facilitate goal attainment. Bemused by the rules, some people may elevate them above organizational goals. One example is the early World War II requirement that naval officers carry calling cards, even when destined for service in the battles of the South Pacific. Another is the denial of citizenship to an explorer, on the grounds that he had been out of the United States for a time, even though his absence involved service on a U.S. expedition to Antarctica. It is such mistaken emphasis on rules that leads to the association of bureaucracy with red tape and that creates an image of the bureaucrat as haughty or niggling.

Thus, stated briefly, the great danger for formal organizations is that, in their desire to make sure that certain means are taken care of, persons will lose sight of the ends to which these means are meant to contribute. The person who gets caught up in his work or excited about his particular activity must be careful lest he forget what the organization is all about.

We do not imply, of course, that only those persons whose activities contribute directly to goal attainment contribute to the organization. All persons with specific assignments in the division of labor contribute. Nevertheless, insofar as participants are grouped into departments or other units, each of which has subgoals or targets, their activities are essentially halfway stations on the road to the over-all organizational goals.

The Problem of Support

In no organization can participants spend all their time on goal attainment. At least some, and perhaps a great deal, must be spent on activities which do not make even an indirect contribution.

To illustrate, in task-oriented small groups, under laboratory conditions, two major sets of processes operate.[12] On being

---

[12] See Robert Bales, "Task Roles and Social Roles in Problem-Solving Groups," in *Readings in Social Psychology,* ed. Eleanor F. Maccoby, Theodore M. Newcomb, and Eugene L. Hartley (New York: Henry Holt, 1958), pp. 437–47.

assigned a particular task or goal, groups typically begin by giving their attention to the most efficient way of moving toward the goal, which consists of solutions to various problems. Very quickly, however, other kinds of activities appear. When someone proposes a given approach, others agree, disagree, or take no stand, and this activity begins to divide the group on the basis of estimates of the most worthwhile approaches. As a consequence of such cleavages, group members develop feelings toward one another or toward the solutions proposed (e.g., irritation at not having their views taken properly into account or simple fatigue). The group must then stop its goal-directed activity and attempt to repair the social damage done as it moves toward the solution of the problem. A kind of "maintenance" activity is necessary, with certain persons assuming the role of "maintenance engineers" in giving attention to social-emotional needs. Persons who have worked with conference groups and other kinds of task-oriented groups are well aware that some time must always be given to informal chit-chat and laughter or other kinds of behavior related to solidarity or to satisfaction of personal needs.

Paradoxically, an organization must do more than give attention to goal attainment in order to attain its goals. It is noteworthy that in one attempt to state a set of conditions necessary to system survival, the categories of adaptation, integration, pattern-maintenance, and tension-management, as well as goal attainment, are named.[13] A good part of any system's energies must be spent on activities that do not contribute directly to goal attainment but rather are concerned with maintaining the system itself.

There is a tendency in various units in an organization to exaggerate the importance of their own contribution and to think of the whole organization in terms of the goals of the particular unit. Such an attitude comes close to what is called the bureaucratic personality. Thus, the head of the section concerned with providing the rivets used in a large manufacturing operation begins to think of the making of rivets as an end in itself and forgets that they are a means for making some other product. Yet it is essential that he believe that making rivets is the most important thing in the world and that he give his full attention to this task, rather than questioning what rivets contribute to the

[13] Parsons *et al.* (eds.), *Theories of Society.*

over-all organization.[14] Here we have something close to a craft or professional orientation. One of the functions of making the craftsman or professional independent is to free him from the necessity of being concerned with the uses to which his skills are put, so that he can concentrate on the maximum development of those skills. Only in this manner can he make a major contribution.

In other words, an organization must to some extent insulate its units so that they need not give attention to goals other than their particular concerns. This is not to say that each unit should be given its head and that the purposes of an organization are well served if all its members are bureaucratic personalities. Cognizance must be taken, however, of activities which may be only indirectly related, or even unrelated, to organizational goals. The same reasoning applies to activities which are wholly of a supportive character, in the sense in which we have been using the term: that is, those activities that involve adaptation, integration, pattern-maintenance, and tension-management. If such activities are to be carried out effectively, the persons concerned with them must make ends of these means. And when a means becomes an end, it has also become a goal of the organization.

In short, any organization has two kinds of goals: those which are manifested in a product of some kind and which we shall call "output goals" and those which are the ends of persons responsible for the maintenance activities, which we shall call "support goals."

DEVELOPMENT OF THE RESEARCH INSTRUMENT

The basic source of the data used in this study was a mailed questionnaire, supplemented by interviews, a survey of the literature, and various sources of information on institutions. The questionnaire included, among other items, a list of 47 goals, developed in accordance with the rationale just outlined: that is, that in any organization, activities concerned with support may be regarded as goals, since they are essential to the healthy functioning of the organization; since they clearly involve an intention or aim of the organization as a whole; and since many par-

[14] A comparable situation exists in many universities. Each department tries to outdo all others in its search for resources to take care of its own needs. As we point out later, one of the goals that our respondents were asked to rate involved the question of whether they should try to maintain top quality in *all* the university's programs. In view of limited resources, such an emphasis would seem to invite the war of each against the other.

ticipants perceive them as worthy, give a great deal of attention to them, and deliberately engage in activities that will move the organization toward them. With respect to the situation in which means become ends, we assert that the success of the organization depends on that process's taking place. It represents an organizational dysfunction only when nonoutput goals are substituted for output goals to such an extent that a sizable number of persons devote themselves only to nonoutput goals. In such a situation, the bureaucratic personality has taken over. It should be pointed out that the opposite process is also possible. That is, people may insist that output goals be considered exclusively and that support goals be ignored. This approach is usually criticized as "unrealistic" and "ivory-towerish."

Two kinds of evidence are necessary before one can confidently assert that a goal is present: intentions and activities. By *intentions*, we refer to what participants see the organization as trying to do: what they believe its goals to be, what direction they feel it is taking as an organization. Intentions are revealed either by verbal statements or by inferences made from symbolic acts, gestures, and other types of meaningful behavior. By *activities*, we refer to what persons in the organization are in fact observed to be doing: how they are spending their time, how resources are being allocated.

This approach can be illustrated by a simple example. If we are to conclude that a person's goal is to go through an open doorway, two kinds of evidence are necessary. First, we may ask him what it is that he intends to do and he may reply that he intends to walk through the doorway. But it is possible, of course, that he is lying or that he himself is not sure what he intends to do. Hence, in addition to his statement, we must also observe his behavior. When his behavior, if continued, would seem to have at least a modest probability of moving him toward the door and if he seems to be looking toward the door and moving his feet in the direction of the door, then we may reasonably conclude that such indeed is his goal.

Both intentions and activities must be distinguished from *outputs*, which the organization produces or distributes to persons or systems outside itself. In the case of the university, there may be strong consensus that a major university goal is preparing students for useful careers (an intention), but members of the faculty may be observed to spend much of their time in research instead (an activity), and a relatively high proportion of the student body may get degrees in the liberal arts (an output). Thus the three components do not necessarily correspond. Before one can confidently speak of a goal, there must be some degree of correspondence between intentions and activities. On the other hand, evidence about outputs refers not to goal activity as such, but rather to the organization's success in goal attainment.

It would have been desirable to include data on activities and outputs. Because of the large number of universities in our sample, however, such data proved to be too highly variable to allow for comparisons among institutions. Some universities keep careful records of how professors spend their time; others regard even asking the question as an interference with academic freedom. In other cases, data were good only for certain years. Since we had close to 10,000 respondents, even sampling would not have been feasible. In the end, we gave up the attempt to secure such information.

Our findings, then, are based solely on statements of goal intentions. We believe, however, that they give an adequate representation of goals for the following reasons:

First, each person was asked to state whether he thought a given goal *was* important (that is, strongly emphasized) at his university. Then, on the following line of the questionnaire, he was asked whether he thought it *should be* important. This distinction gave some protection against the danger that his perceptions of actual goals would be simply an expression of his own goal preferences.

Second, we decided that a given goal was of a certain degree of importance at a particular university by taking the average of the perceptions of all the respondents—both faculty and administrators—at that university. Each person was asked to check a response indicating his perception of its importance. The response was scored on a scale from 1 to 5, and the mean for the institution derived. Then the standard deviation was calculated, and if it exceeded 1—that is, if consensus on the rank of the goal was low—we considered the mean to be an untrustworthy indication of the goal's true position at a given university. Although some respondents may not have opportunity to observe the actual importance of a goal, most probably do, and it is a fair assumption that the average is a reasonable estimate of what rank the goal has. One can, of course, recall Samuel Johnson's observation that an average of the opinion of gossips is still gossip, but we believe we are not summarizing gossip here. We did not ask for second-hand opinions, but for perceptions. In effect, we asked Professor X or Dean Y at the University of A to act as our eyes, saying, "We cannot come to the University of A to check on how you actually spend your time. So we ask you to look for us and give us a report on what you have seen." We calculated the average not because it unquestionably represents reality, but because it is more probable that a large number of observers will come close to the truth than that a large number will err and only a few be on target.

Finally, we are reasonably confident that statements of goal intentions correspond with actual goals because our respondents were, after all, full-time employees of the university they reported on. Further, since we tried to survey all administrators and a 10 percent sample of faculty members, we have data on the perceptions of persons throughout the university. Their combined view should be reasonably revealing. What has been said here does not apply, of course, to their responses about what the goals ought to be. In that instance, we were asking for opinions—or, more accurately, for expressions of attitudes and values.

The List of Goal Intentions

As indicated previously, we found it useful to describe the goals of a university in terms of categories designating the functional imperatives of social systems, modified to apply directly to organizations. We thus identified a total of 47 goals. Even this long list is by no means comprehensive; the goals are intended to represent the several major categories. It must be borne in mind that they apply to universities only, and not to other types of higher educational institutions. Further, most of them will be present to some extent in all universities; it is the emphasis that each receives, relative to other goals, in which we are interested. By developing a rank order of goals, we emerged with a *goal structure* for each university.

The goals are classified under two major headings: Output goals—subdivided into Student-Expressive, Student-Instrumental, Research, and Direct Service goals—and Support goals—subdivided into Adaptation, Management, Motivation, and Position goals.

OUTPUT GOALS

Output goals are those goals of the university which, immediately or in the future, are reflected in some product, service, skill, or orientation which will affect (and is intended to affect) society.

Student-Expressive goals involve the attempt to change the student's identity or character in some fundamental way.
1. Produce a student who, whatever else may be done to him, has had his intellect cultivated to the maximum.
2. Produce a well-rounded student, that is, one whose physical, social, moral, intellectual, and esthetic potentialities have all been cultivated.
3. Make sure the student is permanently affected (in mind and spirit) by the great ideas of the great minds of history.
4. Assist students to develop objectivity about themselves and their beliefs and hence examine those beliefs critically.
5. Develop the inner character of students so that they can make sound, correct moral choices.

Student-Instrumental goals involve the student's being equipped to do something specific for the society which he will be entering or to operate in a specific way in that society.
6. Prepare students specifically for useful careers.
7. Provide the student with skills, attitudes, contacts, and experiences which maximize the likelihood of his occupying a high status in life and a position of leadership in society.
8. Train students in methods of scholarship and/or scientific research and/or creative endeavor.
9. Make a good consumer of the student—a person who is elevated culturally, has good taste, and can make good consumer choices.
10. Produce a student who is able to perform his citizenship responsibilities effectively.

Research goals involve the production of new knowledge or the solution of problems.
11. Carry on pure research.
12. Carry on applied research.

Direct Service goals involve the direct and continuing provision of services to the population outside the university (that is, not faculty, full-time students, or staff). These services are provided because the university, as an organization, is better equipped than any other organization to provide them.

13. Provide special training for part-time adult students, through extension courses, special short courses, correspondence courses, etc.

14. Assist citizens directly through extension programs, advice, consultation, and the provision of useful or needed facilities and services other than teaching.

15. Provide cultural leadership for the community through university-sponsored programs in the arts, public lectures by distinguished persons, athletic events, and other performances, displays, or celebrations which present the best of culture, popular or not.

16. Serve as a center for the dissemination of new ideas that will change the society, whether those ideas are in science, literature, the arts, or politics.

17. Serve as a center for the preservation of the cultural heritage.

SUPPORT GOALS

Adaptation goals reflect the need for the university as an organization to come to terms with the environment in which it is located: to attract students and staff, to finance the enterprise, to secure needed resources, and to validate the activities of the university with those persons or agencies in a position to affect them.

18. Ensure the continued confidence and hence support of those who contribute substantially (other than students and recipients of services) to the finances and other material resource needs of the university.

19. Ensure the favorable appraisal of those who validate the quality of the programs we offer (validating groups include accrediting bodies, professional societies, scholarly peers at other universities, and respected persons in intellectual or artistic circles).

20. Educate to his utmost capacities every high school graduate who meets basic legal requirements for admission.

21. Accommodate only students of high potential in terms of the specific strengths and emphases of this university.

22. Orient ourselves to the satisfaction of the special needs and problems of the immediate geographical region.

23. Keep costs down as low as possible, through more efficient utilization of time and space, reduction of course duplication, etc.
24. Hold our staff in the face of inducements offered by other universities.

Management goals involve decisions on who should run the university, the need to handle conflict, and the establishment of priorities as to which output goals should be given maximum attention.

25. Make sure that salaries, teaching assignments, perquisites, and privileges always reflect the contribution that the person involved is making to his own profession or discipline.
26. Involve faculty in the government of the university.
27. Involve students in the government of the university.
28. Make sure the university is run democratically insofar as that is feasible.
29. Keep harmony between departments or divisions of the university when such departments or divisions do not see eye to eye on important matters.
30. Make sure that salaries, teaching assignments, perquisites, and privileges always reflect the contribution that the person involved is making to the functioning of this university.
31. Emphasize undergraduate instruction even at the expense of the graduate program.
32. Encourage students to go into graduate work.
33. Make sure the university is run by those selected according to their ability to attain the goals of the university in the most efficient manner possible.
34. Make sure that on *all* important issues (not only curriculum), the will of the full-time faculty shall prevail.

Motivation goals seek to ensure a high level of satisfaction on the part of staff and students and emphasize loyalty to the university as a whole.

35. Protect the faculty's right to academic freedom.
36. Make this a place in which faculty have maximum opportunity to pursue their careers in a manner satisfactory to them by their own criteria.
37. Provide a full round of student activities.
38. Protect and facilitate the students' right to inquire into, in-

vestigate, and examine critically any idea or program that they might get interested in.

39. Protect and facilitate the students' right to advocate direct action of a political or social kind and any attempts on their part to organize efforts to attain political or social goals.
40. Develop loyalty on the part of the faculty and staff to the university, rather than only to their own jobs or professional concerns.
41. Develop greater pride on the part of faculty, staff, and students in their university and the things it stands for.

Position goals help to maintain the position of the university in terms of the kind of place it is compared with other universities and in the face of trends which could change its position.

42. Maintain top quality in all programs we engage in.
43. Maintain top quality in those programs we feel to be especially important (other programs being, of course, up to acceptable standards).
44. Maintain a balanced level of quality across the whole range of programs we engage in.
45. Keep up to date and responsive.
46. Increase the prestige of the university or, if you believe it is already extremely high, ensure the maintenance of that prestige.
47. Keep this place from becoming something different from what it is now; that is, preserve its peculiar emphases and point of view, its "character."

It is our belief that the study of organizations has suffered from an oversimple view of goals. Most organizations are characterized as having but one goal, and the many past classifications that reflect this notion have proved most unhelpful in that they tell little about the organizations they purport to describe. A goal structure, with ranked goals, seems much more valuable.

Organizations undoubtedly differ in the complexity of their goal structures, those of universities being among the more complex. The American university is probably unique in the number of its output goals, though the structure of its support goals may be less complex than that of other organizations. A manufacturing firm, in contrast, may have a very short list of output goals and a long list of support goals, depending on its problems with management, with supplies, and with competition.

Only slightly more than one-third of the goals on our list are output goals,[15] even though they are what people usually have in mind when they discuss an organization's goals. But, to repeat our earlier contention, it is possible for any activity to become an organizational goal, even repairing broken plumbing, provided it is conceived of as an organizational problem. Goals may and do change over time, but some kind of adaptation, management, motivation, and position goals will always be present in every organization.

To illustrate how support goals function in the university, the adaptation goal "Ensure the continued confidence and hence support of those who contribute substantially . . . to the finances and other material resource needs of the university" may be ranked high in many universities, and respondents at the university may agree on this high ranking. A person may say that this goal is emphasized because of remarks he hears, because of statements he reads in the university catalogue, because of what he observes of administrative activities, or because of his awareness that there is a general concern among faculty and others to behave in public situations so as to represent the university in an honorable manner and a tendency to criticize persons who engage in behavior which secures unfavorable public attention.

We see no useful purpose in insisting that this goal is, after all, a means which enables the university to pursue its output goals. This point is true, but ensuring the confidence of contributors is no less a goal for that. Deliberate attention is given to it by the entire university, just as deliberate attention is given to the goals of providing direct service to the community and of teaching students. The same will be true of such management goals as making sure that the university is run democratically, such motivation goals as protecting the faculty's right to academic freedom, and such position goals as maintaining the character of the university. Indeed, the claim could be made that output goals are a means for the attainment of position goals. For example, only by producing students of a certain kind can the

---

[15] The relative numbers of output and support goals are arbitrary. We do not mean to suggest that more time is spent on support than on output activities or that there are more kinds of support activities than output activities. Either list could presumably be lengthened or shortened.

university continue to preserve its peculiar emphases and point of view, its "character."

Finer distinctions could be made. For example, persons who give heavy emphasis to management goals, to the neglect of adaptation goals, may be said to have an insular orientation: They ignore the place of the university in the community, the environment in which it must do business to survive. Persons who insist that every attention be given to maintaining the top quality of a particular university may be guilty of what Caplow has called "organizational aggrandizement," [16] whereas persons who stress motivation goals may be regarded as believing that the university exists only to satisfy the needs of those in it, rather than to serve society.

It should be remembered that respondents were asked not only about their observations as to what the goals of their universities actually are (thus producing a rank ordering of *perceived goals*), but also about what they felt those goals should be (thus producing a rank ordering of *preferred goals*). The 47 goals were randomly mixed as to content in the questionnaire itself (see *Appendix C,* page 133).

Other Information Included in the Questionnaire

As a glance at *Appendix C* will show, the questionnaire was long, and much of the information it asked for is not relevant to this report. Some other items of information, however, were utilized in this investigation of goals.

Since we predicted that goals would be related to power structure, one section of the questionnaire dealt with the respondent's perception of what persons or groups make the big decisions at his institution. Specifically, respondents were asked how much influence in decision making was exerted by the following groups: trustees, legislators, sources of large private grants or endowments, Federal government agencies, state government agencies, the president, the vice-president, the dean of the graduate school, the dean of liberal arts, the deans of professional schools, chairmen of departments, faculty, students, parents, citizens of the state, and alumni. (See Section #2 of *Appendix C,* page 143.)

In addition, we asked questions about age, sex, education, and so forth, in an effort to discover whether such factors affect

---

[16] Theodore Caplow, *Principles of Organization* (New York: Harcourt, Brace, and World, 1964), pp. 213–16.

the values people hold with reference to university goals and whether administrators and faculty members differ substantially in their backgrounds and personal characteristics.

SAMPLE DESIGN, RESPONSE RATE, AND STATISTICAL TESTS

Because we focused on special organizational problems, particularly situations in which administrators and faculty members might strongly disagree on goal definition, and because we were interested in whether such goal conflict was related to the power structure of the university, we decided to restrict our study to the educational institutions most likely to exhibit such conflict and to vary among themselves in power structure.

In many types of institution (for example, small, church-controlled liberal arts colleges for men), consensus about organizational goals and values is probably almost complete. Hence, we deliberately excluded institutions dominated by some single point of view or value commitment which would severely limit goal variation. Not included in the design of the study, therefore, were church-controlled institutions, liberal arts colleges, teachers colleges, and technical institutions.

Our population consisted of the nondenominational universities in the United States,[17] the institutions that seem most likely to exhibit goal variation. Moreover, it is often claimed that support functions have increased greatly and administrators have attained too much power in the universities. Finally, for our purposes, it was necessary that the institution have a graduate school, to ensure that the goal of research would be well represented.

Institutions were selected on the basis of the following five criteria:

1. The Ph.D. degree or its equivalent must be offered.
2. The Ph.D. degree must be granted in at least three of the four major disciplinary areas (humanities, biological sciences, physical sciences, and social sciences).
3. The degrees granted in the two least emphasized fields must come to 10 percent or more of the total degrees con-

---

[17] Our study also included nine denominational (mostly Catholic) universities which met our criteria for universities in all respects. Preliminary analysis indicated, however, that they made up a universe of their own and deserved separate tabulation and analysis. Consequently we are not reporting on them here.

ferred. This provision was designed to avoid any undue concentration in one field and thus to help ensure a diversity of goals.

4. The institution must have a liberal arts undergraduate school with three or more professional schools.
5. The institution must have conferred ten or more degrees during the years 1962–63.

The ninth edition of *American Universities and Colleges* [18] was our source of information about the 70 institutions selected. Two of these—the University of Minnesota and the University of Washington—were excluded, because they were the home institutions of the investigators and because the University of Minnesota was used for a pretest. The remaining 68 universities were substantially the same as those in Berelson's study of graduate institutions [19] (with denominational, technical, and starred universities excluded), except for the addition of a few institutions which had attained university status since Berelson's list was compiled.

NOTE.—Readers who are not interested in sampling procedures and an analysis of response rates may wish to skip the following section and turn to page 24, "Organization of the Book."

Drawing the sample of respondents presented a number of problems. We had decided to send questionnaires to all administrators (department chairmen, deans, vice-presidents, presidents and their staff) and to a 10 percent sample of the faculty at each of the 68 universities. Our reasoning was that though the total number of administrators is large, the number in particular categories is small; if it were too small, comparisons between different categories would be difficult. The number of faculty, on the other hand, is sufficiently large so that a 10 percent sampling would be representative. On the basis of the best information we were able to obtain, our figures for the 68 universities in the spring of 1964 were: administrators, 8,828; faculty, 67,560. With a 10

[18] Allan M. Cartter (ed.), *American Universities and Colleges,* 9th ed. (Washington: American Council on Education, 1964). Purdue University turned out to be an exception. It was not classified as a university in the volume, yet we felt that it was excluded by a minor technicality. Consequently, we included it in our sample. Such places as MIT and Caltech are automatically excluded by our criteria.

[19] Bernard Berelson, *Graduate Education in the United States* (New York: McGraw-Hill Book Co., 1960), pp. 280–82.

percent sample of the faculty (6,756), the total sample numbered 15,584.

Questionnaires were mailed out in late spring of 1964. Unfortunately, the timing was poor—just before commencement, when administrators as well as faculty are busy—and then, during the summer, of course, many potential respondents were simply not on campus. Six weeks after the first mailing, a follow-up postcard was sent out. Approximately three months later, a second mailing of the questionnaire was sent to all non-respondents; and, in addition, the investigators made personal pleas to some. In short, a member of the sample might have been approached as many as four times. Questionnaires kept coming in for as long as a year after the first mailing.

From the beginning, we faced the problem common to all mail surveys: a low response rate. Adding to this difficulty, the questionnaire was a long one, taking a minimum of an hour and a half to complete. (Some respondents wrote that they had spent as long as three hours on it.) Moreover, university personnel, particularly administrators, are jaded with questionnaires.[20]

Anticipating resistance, therefore, we employed a number of devices to increase the response rate. We solicited help from various accrediting bodies and professional organizations, asking them to lend their support to the study by letting us use their names and by speaking favorably of the study in their own literature; we obtained assistance from 90 members of the American Association of Collegiate Schools of Business; we were given valuable aid by O. Meredith Wilson, President of the University of Minnesota, who kindly agreed to write letters to his fellow presidents at all 68 universities, mentioning his own personal interest in the study and urging them to complete the questionnaire.

The response rate (usable questionnaires) was as follows:

	Administrators	Faculty	TOTAL
Respondents	4,494	2,730	7,224
Nonrespondents	4,334	4,026	8,360
TOTAL	8,828	6,756	15,584
Percent Response	50.9	40.4	46.4

[20] To our surprise, the president of one university not in our sample wrote to us expressing concern that his institution had not been included. It may be that one way in which institutions become recognized as universities is that they join the circuit of places to which questionnaires are sent.

On the whole, we feel confident that we secured an adequate response, given the special conditions under which we were working. The level of response was much higher than is usually the case with mail surveys, particularly long ones. Administrators had a higher response rate than faculty, probably because they were more interested in the outcome of the study and because they had secretarial and other help available.

Response rates for the various administrative categories were as follows: presidents, 42 percent; academic vice-presidents, 56 percent; nonacademic vice-presidents, 42 percent; academic deans, 52 percent; nonacademic deans, 53 percent; directors, 50 percent; chairmen, 51 percent. In general, these percentages are close to the over-all response rate for administrators of 51 percent. That presidents deviated sharply from this figure is to be expected; the chief executive of a university is a busy man and may simply not have the time to complete a questionnaire.

The response rate from public institutions was slightly higher than that from private; perhaps persons at public institutions are more service-oriented and thus more responsive to requests for assistance from outside sources.

Given these small differences in response rate, the question arises as to whether the group which responded was biased in ways which distort the findings. In an attempt to check on possible response bias, we took a random sample of 200 nonrespondents and wrote them special letters asking them to fill out the questionnaire solely for the purpose of serving as controls. If this unique procedure were to work, nearly 100 percent response would have been required—a highly unlikely rate without personal interviews. Unfortunately, the response rate was about the same as it had been in earlier attempts to follow up nonrespondents, so no inferences could be drawn from the analysis.

It is our belief that the respondents were not biased, at least not in ways relevant to the purposes of the study. It could be argued that among the nonrespondents is a small group opposed in principle to questionnaires as a way of acquiring knowledge. Indeed, we received letters from some persons stating this position. One prominent university president wrote us that he was "constitutionally opposed to all questionnaires." Although we know of no data to support the claim, it is conceivable that these same people are opposed to the study of human behavior generally. The bias could be either strongly humanistic or strongly scientific: The humanist might feel that one *should* not study human behavior, his attitude being one of "touch it and the bloom is gone," whereas the natural scientist might feel that one *cannot* study it scientifically and that the material of the social sciences actually belongs in the humanities. Of course, the questionnaire contains no goal dealing with the teaching of the social sciences, but such attitudes might be related to other attitudes about goals: producing a well-rounded student, for instance, or doing pure research. These possibilities are doubtful and totally speculative, but if a bias is operating in our data, it is probably in that direction. On the other hand, as we shall point out in our subsequent discussion, so many of the findings make sense, in that they fit together and have internal congruence, that it is difficult to believe any consistent bias was operating.

A detailed discussion of the techniques of analysis used and the statistical tests applied is given in *Appendix B,* page 124. But a word should be said here about the quantitative index of the degree of association for cross-classified data used throughout this report. "Gamma," which was proposed by Leo A. Goodman and William H. Kruskal,[21] may be roughly compared to the familiar "Pearsonian *r*" or product-moment coefficient of correlation. That is, its value ranges from a possible maximum of 1.00 down through 0 to a possible minimum of -1.00. It is suitable for the kind of analysis of data used to compare the location of an institution in two categories or scales at the same time. In the words of the authors, the value of *gamma* "tells us how much more probable it is to get like than unlike orders in the two classifications. . . ."[22] The value of *gamma* cannot be determined if all the data are concentrated in a single row or column of a cross-tabulation, and the value is zero if there is no association whatever between the two classifications.

A typical cross-classification might be three categories of institutional size and a five-point scale measuring "prestige." If size and prestige were perfectly and positively related, *gamma* would equal 1.00; if there were no relationship between the two, *gamma* would be zero; if size and prestige were always perfectly negatively related (i.e., the smaller the institution, the greater the prestige), the value of *gamma* would be -1.00.

[21] "Measures of Associations for Cross Classifications," *Journal of the American Statistical Association,* December 1954, 732-764.
[22] *Ibid.,* p. 749.

As in the case of any other statistic, *gamma* is subject to sampling errors. The "z" referred to in this report, roughly comparable to a "critical ratio," is used to estimate the probability that a given value could have been as large (regardless of algebraic sign) if its "true" value were zero. If the "z" associated with a given value of *gamma* is too small, the value is usually not even cited and may be thought of as having no statistical significance, in the usual sense. In general, a value of *gamma* is accepted as "significant" in this report if the probability of its being the result of random error or pure chance is very small: i.e., is equal to or less than 5 percent ($p \leq .05$).[23]

Goodman and Kruskal's *gamma* has the further advantage of being adapted to ordinal measures (most of the data have been so arranged) and of measuring the strength (or closeness) of a relationship and not merely its significance. In this respect, it is comparable to r^2 (the squared correlation coefficient) in that a *gamma* of .800 may be regarded as twice as "strong" as one of .400. Such is not the case for most of the commonly used measures of association.

ORGANIZATION OF THE BOOK

This study focuses on the goals of universities, the goal values of the respondents, and the view and attitudes of administrators as compared with those of faculty members. It seeks also to investigate relationships between the goal structure (both perceived and preferred) and other characteristics of the university.

Chapter 2 begins with the over-all view of university goals. Taking the group of respondents as a whole, without reference to the university as a unit, we present data on the rankings of perceived and preferred goals and on the congruence between the two. In this way, one gets a general answer to certain questions. In the view of faculty and administrators, do American universities seem to be headed in the right direction? Do the respondents feel that what *is* comes close to what *ought* to be? The chapter also discusses the extent of goal congruence at particular universities, in order to discover whether a state of harmony and satisfaction or one of discord and tension generally exists at our universities.

[23] Those interested in the sampling theory may wish to refer to another paper by Goodman and Kruskal, "Measures of Association for Cross Classification: III. Approximate Sampling Theory," *Journal of the American Statistical Association,* June 1963, 310–364.

In Chapter 3, we explore the relationship between the university's goal structure and certain of its global characteristics: size, location, type of control, productivity, prestige, and graduate emphasis.

We take up the problem of the power structure of universities in Chapter 4. The subject is of intrinsic interest. Moreover, it stands to reason that the groups who have the most power are also those whose values and attitudes will determine goal emphases. First, an over-all picture of the power of various persons and groups is drawn. Second, power structure is related to the global characteristics considered in the previous chapter. And finally, the relationship between power structure and perceived goals is investigated.

In Chapter 5, the question of whether administrators and faculty members differ in their personal and background characteristics is investigated. Further, their attitudes and values as reflected in their perceived and preferred goal structures are compared. Our interest here was in seeing if there is any justification to the charge that the greater power of administrators poses a threat to the scholarly and other interests of faculty members.

The final chapter summarizes the preceding discussion and underscores the major findings of the study with respect to the goals of American universities and the possible determinants of those goals.

CHAPTER 2

GOAL CONGRUENCE AND DISSONANCE IN UNIVERSITIES

What do our respondents think the goals of American universities (1) are and (2) ought to be? This chapter deals with these two questions and with discrepancies between the perceived and the preferred goals of the total group of respondents. After the over-all picture has been sketched, two further analyses —across universities and within university—are introduced to identify more precisely areas of harmony and discord with respect to goals at particular institutions.

THE OVER-ALL PICTURE

For each of the 47 goals listed on the questionnaire, respondents were asked to indicate (1) how important they felt the goal actually was at their university and (2) how important they felt it should be. They used a five-point scale, ranging from 5 ("absolutely top importance") down to 1 ("no importance"). (See *Appendix C*, page 135.) The mean score for each particular goal was derived by calculating the mean at each university and then calculating the mean of the adjusted institutional means. The results of this analysis are shown in *Table 1*,[1] which indicates also the rank order and the standard deviation for each goal. The number of responses on which these figures are based varies from one goal to another, since some persons skipped questions and others answered ambiguously by checking more than one alternative or by writing in comments that cast doubt on the alternative they did check. The extent of deviation in this respect was small.

Perceived Goals

The goals actually being pursued at American universities are listed in rank order in *Table 1* under the heading "Perceived Goals." The standard deviation suggests the degree of consensus about the emphasis given to a particular goal: The lower the

[1] *Appendix A* provides a key to the abbreviated version of goal statements that are used in the tables. *See* page 118.

standard deviation, the more confident we can be that the mean score represents true agreement about the position of the goal rather than an averaging of widely divergent high and low scores. In general, respondents seem in accord about the relative emphasis given to particular goals. In only six instances—educating to the utmost each high school graduate who meets the basic legal requirements for admission, preserving the special character of the university, accepting only those students with high potential, running the university democratically, providing special training for part-time adult students, and satisfying regional needs—did the standard deviation exceed .90. All but one—providing special training—are support goals; apparently there is considerable

TABLE 1

THE GOALS OF AMERICAN UNIVERSITIES

GOAL	PERCEIVED			PREFERRED		
	Rank	Mean	Standard Deviation	Rank	Mean	Standard Deviation
35. Protect academic freedom...	1	3.90	.83	1	4.33	.74
46. Increase or maintain prestige.	2	3.76	.71	11	3.80	.74
43. Maintain top quality in important programs........	3	3.69	.73	7	3.99	.72
18. Ensure confidence of contributors..................	4	3.66	.76	26	3.52	.84
45. Keep up to date...........	5	3.57	.76	6	4.09	.67
8. Train students for scholarship/research...........	6	3.56	.76	2	4.17	.62
11. Carry on pure research......	7	3.55	.83	16	3.76	.80
42. Maintain top quality in all programs...............	8	3.49	.81	4	4.14	.72
19. Ensure favor of validating bodies.................	9	3.43	.79	34	3.31	.89
33. Ensure efficient goal attainment..................	10	3.42	.85	9	3.99	.78
16. Disseminate new ideas......	11	3.39	.85	5	4.10	.77
12. Carry on applied research....	12	3.39	.80	30	3.37	.85
6. Prepare students for useful careers.................	13	3.39	.72	32	3.34	.81
1. Cultivate student's intellect..	14	3.38	.79	3	4.17	.75
24. Hold staff in face of inducements..................	15	3.37	.75	18	3.74	.75
15. Provide community cultural leadership..............	16	3.33	.73	28	3.49	.76
38. Protect students' right of inquiry.................	17	3.31	.86	10	3.88	.82
32. Encourage graduate work....	18	3.30	.68	27	3.51	.66
17. Preserve cultural heritage....	19	3.28	.82	20	3.63	.84
10. Prepare student for citizenship....................	20	3.27	.76	14	3.76	.77
2. Produce well-rounded student	21	3.25	.78	17	3.75	.87
36. Give faculty maximum opportunity to pursue careers.	22	3.22	.78	25	3.55	.85

agreement about the output goals currently emphasized.

If we mark off at the top those goals whose means fall within approximately one standard deviation of the entire distribution, we may define the seven top goals of American universities. They are in order:

1. Protect the faculty's right to academic freedom.
2. Increase or maintain the prestige of the university.
3. Maintain top quality in those programs felt to be especially important.
4. Ensure the continued confidence and hence support of

TABLE 1 *continued*

GOAL	PERCEIVED			PREFERRED		
	Rank	Mean	Standard Deviation	Rank	Mean	Standard Deviation
4. Develop student's objectivity	23	3.22	.82	8	3.99	.69
23. Keep costs down............	24	3.22	.76	35	3.30	.79
26. Involve faculty in university government..............	25	3.21	.88	19	3.63	.83
25. Reward for contribution to profession..............	26	3.20	.75	21	3.63	.77
37. Provide student activities....	27	3.19	.76	43	2.99	.85
7. Prepare students for status/ leadership..............	28	3.18	.78	33	3.31	.96
28. Run university democratically	29	3.16	.91	22	3.61	.88
3. Affect student with great ideas....................	30	3.16	.80	15	3.76	.82
14. Assist citizens through extension programs...........	31	3.10	.86	36	3.22	.89
30. Reward for contribution to institution..............	32	3.10	.74	13	3.77	.74
41. Develop pride in university...	33	3.09	.77	23	3.59	.81
22. Satisfy area needs..........	34	3.07	.90	42	3.00	.92
44. Maintain balanced quality in all programs.............	35	3.07	.82	31	3.36	.96
34. Let will of faculty prevail....	36	3.01	.84	24	3.56	.83
13. Provide special adult training.	37	3.00	.90	38	3.18	.88
5. Develop student's character..	38	2.95	.85	12	3.79	.89
20. Educate to utmost high school graduates........	39	2.93	1.07	37	3.19	1.26
21. Accept good students only...	40	2.89	.96	39	3.09	.96
39. Protect students' right of action.................	41	2.88	.86	40	3.08	.97
40. Develop faculty loyalty to institution..............	42	2.86	.79	29	3.47	.88
29. Keep harmony............	43	2.84	.79	41	3.06	.90
31. Emphasize undergraduate instruction................	44	2.66	.89	44	2.89	1.04
27. Involve students in university government..........	45	2.60	.85	46	2.69	.94
47. Preserve institutional character....................	46	2.56	.98	47	2.13	.99
9. Cultivate student's taste....	47	2.47	.84	45	2.78	1.05

those who contribute substantially to the finances and other material resource needs of the university.

5. Keep up to date and responsive.
6. Train students in methods of scholarship and/or scientific research and/or creative endeavor.
7. Carry on pure research.

Most striking is the prominence given to the goal of protecting the academic freedom of the faculty: In addition, at all universities in the sample, this goal was ranked in the top third. Apparently, administrators and faculty who participated in the study feel that, right now, this goal is being pursued before all others.

A second remarkable characteristic is that only one of the seven goals is concerned in any way with students, and that one —the output goal of training students for research and scholarship—is closely associated with the scholarly interests of professors and with the emphasis given to pure research. The singular scarcity of student-oriented goals in the top group is all the more startling when one considers that 18 of the 47 goals listed in the questionnaire refer directly to students. Apparently the current complaint that universities give little attention to the interests of students has considerable basis in fact.

Five of the seven goals on the list are support goals, and the one other ouput goal—carrying on pure research—ranks seventh. Three of the top five support goals have to do with maintaining the university's position in relation to other universities, but no other pattern is evident.

The four lowest-ranked goals (from the bottom up) are:

1. Make a good consumer of the student—a person who is elevated culturally, has good taste, and can make good consumer choices.
2. Keep the university from becoming something different from what it is now; that is, preserve its peculiar emphases and point of view, its "character."
3. Involve students in the government of the university.
4. Emphasize undergraduate instruction even at the expense of the graduate program.

That three of the four lowest-ranked goals are directly concerned with the student underscores the implication that universities tend to take the education of the student for granted. The relative lack of emphasis accorded to undergraduate instruction is consistent with the emphasis on pure research and on training students for scholarship. The second low-ranked goal—preserving institutional character—is somewhat surprising, since the literature of higher education frequently asserts that the diversity of the American system of higher education and the integrity of its individual institutions are among its unique strengths. Perhaps if colleges had been included in the sample, this goal would have ranked higher.

In general, we may say that American universities emphasize the faculty's academic freedom, concern themselves primarily with goals relating to pure research and with maintaining or enhancing the university's position, and manifest relatively little interest in the student beyond developing his scholarly abilities.

Preferred Goals

Respondents were asked to indicate not only what emphasis they felt each goal was actually given, but also what emphasis they felt it should be given. The result was a rank ordering of the preferred goals for the total sample. As the standard deviations in *Table 1* indicate, there was less consensus about preferred goals than about perceived goals. On three—educating to the utmost all legally qualified high school graduates, making a good consumer of the student, and emphasizing undergraduate instruction—disagreement was sharp (standard deviation over 1.0), indicating that the mean score is probably not by itself a trustworthy index of the ratings which these goals received. Eight other goals had standard deviations of .90 or above: preserving the special character of the university, protecting the students' right to direct action, accepting only those students with high potential, preparing the student for high status and a position of leadership, maintaining a balanced level of quality in all programs, involving students in university government, satisfying regional needs, and keeping harmony between parts of the university.

Again, the goals on which there is disagreement fall into the lowest third of the total distribution and tend to be support goals. Only two of the eleven—making a good consumer of the student and preparing him for high status and leadership—are output goals. It is also worth noting that seven of the goals relate directly to students: It seems that while most administrators and faculty members place little value on these student-oriented goals, a few tend to rate them high as preferred goals.

Using the same procedure as was used for the perceived goals, we identified nine top preferred goals:

1. Protect the faculty's right to academic freedom.
2. Train students in methods of scholarship and/or scientific research and/or creative endeavor.
3. Produce a student who has had his intellect cultivated to the maximum.
4. Maintain top quality in all programs engaged in.
5. Serve as a center for the dissemination of new ideas.
6. Keep up to date and responsive.
7. Maintain top quality in those programs felt to be especially important.
8. Assist students to develop objectivity about themselves and their beliefs and hence examine those beliefs critically.
9. Make sure the university is run by those selected according to their ability to attain the goals of the university in the most efficient manner possible.

As with the perceived goals, the goal of protecting the faculty's academic freedom heads the list: In this case, the actual seems to accord with the ideal. Students come out a little better in the top preferred goals: Preparing the student for scholarship and research (which was, of course, on the list of top perceived goals) and cultivating his intellect rank second and third, and assisting students to develop objectivity and the ability to examine their beliefs critically ranks eighth.

The three lowest-ranked preferred goals (counting from the bottom up) are:

1. Keep the institution from becoming something different from what it is now; that is, preserve its peculiar emphases and point of view, its "character."
2. Involve students in the government of the university.
3. Make a good consumer of the student—a person who is elevated culturally, has good taste, and can make good consumer choices.

All three are also ranked lowest among the perceived goals; the respondents seem to feel, in short, that the relative lack of emphasis given to preserving the university's character and to making the student a good consumer and giving him a voice in the government of the university is entirely appropriate. It may be inferred that those students who seek a greater share of the decision-making power at the university will not receive much support from administrators and faculty. (It should be remembered that these data were collected in 1964 and 1965, prior to the most vigorous student protest and the more constructive student efforts to participate more fully in university governance; it would be interesting to find out how attitudes have changed since then.) Students might take some consolation from the fact that there is no particularly strong feeling that the faculty should be involved in the government of the university: That goal had a mean score of 3.63 and was ranked nineteenth.

To summarize: Students as a group were not felt to be particularly important when respondents were asked about the actual goals of the universities, nor is there evidence of any strong feeling that this state of affairs is unfortunate, except in the case of cultivating the student's intellect and developing his objectivity, both of which, according to our respondents, should receive more emphasis. The perceived and the preferred student-oriented goals which rank at the top relate to the intellective/academic capacities and development of the student; the Renaissance concept of cultivating the whole man is apparently no longer esteemed as an ideal. The findings suggest that preparing students for useful careers or for high status and leadership and developing their citizenship abilities, consumer tastes, characters, or over-all potential (well-roundedness) are not—and should not be—emphasized.

Goal Congruence

Having discussed the relative rankings of the perceived and preferred goals, we can turn our attention to the relation between the two in order to discover how close the actual situation in the American university comes to the ideal, as conceived by our respondents. Although such analysis will not reveal the tensions that may exist at particular universities, it will give a general picture of whether the goals currently being pursued seem to administrators and faculty members to be meaningful and worthwhile and of the discrepancies between perceived and preferred goals in the university system as a whole.

As was mentioned previously, the three lowest-ranked perceived goals are also among the lowest-ranked preferred goals; here, then, the ideal is congruent with the actual. In addition, four of the seven goals rated as those most emphasized are also among those regarded as worthy of emphasis: protecting academic freedom; maintaining top quality in programs felt to be especially important; keeping up to date and responsive; and training students in methods of scholarship, scientific research, and creative endeavor. On the whole, these correspondences are impressive evidence that, at least at the extremes, things are as they should be, in the eyes of administrators and faculty members.

This happy situation does not prevail throughout the distribution. We can usefully divide incongruences into two types: sins of omission—tendencies to subordinate goals which properly should be emphasized—and sins of commission—tendencies to pursue goals which should be subordinated.

To look first at the sins of omission, we find five goals which, according to our respondents, are not receiving the attention they deserve:

1. Develop loyalty on the part of the faculty and staff to the university, rather than only to their own jobs or professional concerns.
2. Make sure that salaries, teaching assignments, perquisites, and privileges always reflect the contribution that the person involved is making to the functioning of the university.
3. Make sure the student is permanently affected (in mind and spirit) by the great ideas of the great minds of history.
4. Assist students to develop objectivity about themselves and their beliefs and hence examine those beliefs critically.
5. Produce a student who has had his intellect cultivated to the maximum.

Much has been said in the literature of higher education about the professor's growing commitment to his discipline and his professional career at the expense of his loyalty to the institution; the first two goals in the list of sins of omission would seem to substantiate the existence of this tendency and to reflect the administrator's dissatisfaction that the personal ambitions and careers of a highly mobile faculty take precedence over their devotion and contributions to the institution. In addition, the second—basing rewards on the person's contributions to the university rather than to his profession—suggests that those persons who serve on committees and carry out other assignments of direct benefit to the institution feel that they are not sufficiently well recognized. The other goals on this list—all of which fall into the category of student-expressive output goals—remind us of the familiar plaint of the liberal arts person that not enough attention is given to cultivating the student's mind or to helping him develop objectivity and insight into himself.

The sins of commission—those goals which our respondents feel receive too much emphasis—are:

1. Provide a full round of student activities.
2. Orient ourselves to the satisfaction of the special needs and problems of the immediate geographical region.
3. Keep costs down as low as possible through more efficient utilization of time and space, reduction of course duplication, etc.
4. Ensure the favorable appraisal of those who validate the quality of the programs offered.
5. Prepare students specifically for useful careers.
6. Carry on applied research.
7. Encourage students to go into graduate work.
8. Ensure the continued confidence and hence support of those who contribute substantially to the finances and other material resource needs of the university.

Even though providing a full round of student activities ranks only twenty-seventh on the list of perceived goals, there is strong feeling that this small degree of emphasis is too much. In view of the over-all scholarly orientation reflected in this listing of "sins," it is also surprising to find that respondents feel that the goal of encouraging students to go into graduate work is stressed too strongly.

In addition, the list of the goals which our respondents feel receive too much attention is remarkable in that four of the eight mentioned are adaptation goals, which relate to the need of the institution to come to terms with the environment in which it is located. Administrators apparently resent the emphasis that is given to such matters as satisfying regional needs, winning the confidence of validating bodies and contributors, and keeping costs low. Two of the other goals on the list—preparing students specifically for useful careers and doing applied research—are consistent with the interpretation that there is some discontent over having to expend so much energy on goals that are practical in nature and that are to some extent imposed upon the university from outside. On the whole, this picture is consistent with the emphasis we have already noted on academic freedom and on the needs and concerns of the faculty in furthering their own professional careers.

THE SIGNIFICANCE OF GOAL CONGRUENCE

In general, we would assume that where there is a high degree of congruence between perceived and preferred goals, a state of harmony and content will exist. Conversely, where what *is* differs markedly from what the staff feels *should be,* a state of dissatisfaction, tension, and even conflict will exist.

But obviously these assumptions represent an oversimplification; some goals are more important than others—important not in the sense of being more strongly emphasized or more highly valued but in the sense of being so pervasive and meaningful that any discrepancy between the ideal and the actual will probably result in a person's leaving the institution for another that comes closer to his expectations of what a university should be. On the other hand, some goals may be so minor in their effects upon the administrator or faculty member that he can easily tolerate incongruence; he may then stay at the university and attempt to change those goals he finds undesirable. For example, a person may feel very strongly that involving the faculty in the government of the university and emphasizing undergraduate instruction should both receive great emphasis, but though he may remain at an institution where undergraduate instruction is slighted, he may seek employment elsewhere if the university fails to involve the faculty in government.

We have so far presented an over-all picture with respect to perceived goals, preferred goals, and the relationship between the two. But such a rough sketch leaves out the finer shadings. Obviously, goal congruence has little meaning except insofar as the goals emphasized at a given institution are also the goals valued by persons at that institution. In this section, we will examine goal congruence at particular institutions, in order to arrive at a more sophisticated and fruitful understanding of the phenomenon. Specifically, what we want to know is: At universities where a goal is rated as being given considerable emphasis (or medium emphasis or little emphasis), is there also the feeling that the goal should be given considerable emphasis (or medium emphasis or little emphasis), and how strong is the relationship? Moreover, we wish to know: On which goals do we find congruence between perceptions and preferences? Presumably in those situations where there is a statistically significant relationship between perceived goals and preferred goals, most of the respondents at the institution agree not only in their perceptions and preferences but also in the significance they attribute to goal congruence. The underlying assumption here is that when a person feels great frustration and dissatisfaction because of goal incongruence, he will move to another institution, whereas in situations where he is not much troubled by goal incongruence, he will remain. By identifying those goals on which there is strong congruence between perceptions and preferences, we will also be isolating significant goals—significant in the implications they have for the condition of the university, the degree of harmony or discord that exists there.

Two kinds of analyses were used to examine the implications of goal congruence: the first, across universities, involves comparisons of the ratings given to a particular goal at different institutions; the second, within university, involves comparisons of the ratings given to different goals at the same institution. More specifically, in the across-universities analysis, the basic unit is the particular goal. The 68 institutions in the sample were ranked and then trichotomized into a high, medium, and low group on the basis of their mean scores on the goal. Here, a university's rating of a goal is being compared with the ratings given to that goal at other universities. In the within-university analysis, the basic unit is the university. The 47 goals in the study were ranked and then trichotomized into a high, medium, and low group on the basis of the ratings they received at a particular university relative to the ratings given to other goals at the same university. (For a fuller account of the methodology and the statistical tests used, see *Appendix B*, page 124.) It should be pointed out that these two types of analyses are intended to get at the same kind of information; the primary reason for doing both was to reveal as many relationships as possible. Take, for instance, the goal of protecting the faculty's academic freedom, which always ranks in the top third, both as a perceived and as a preferred goal. Had the analysis been confined to within-institution comparisons, this goal would then be a constant and could not be related to other variables. When we compare universities with one another, however, we may find that an institution's mean score on the academic freedom goal—though always high relative to the mean score of other goals at the institution—may be low relative to the mean score given to the goal at another institution. The across-universities analysis reveals such differences and permits us to relate them to other institutional characteristics.

Across-Universities Analysis

Table 2 shows those goal congruences which proved statistically significant ($p \leq .05$) in the analysis comparing the ratings of goals from one institution to another. Of the 47 goals, 25 turned out to be statistically significant: that is, the rating given the perceived goal was commensurate with the rating given the preferred goal. At universities where the goal was seen as being strongly emphasized (i.e., ranking in the high group), there was also a tendency to place a high value on the goal (i.e., to rank it in the high "preferred" group). Conversely, at universities where the perceived goal ranked low, the preferred goal tended to rank low also. The larger the *gamma,* the stronger this tendency.

That such a large number of findings emerged from the analysis confirms the notion that universities tend to be selective in mission and in the types of people they attract. For instance, those universities which emphasize academic freedom as a goal (relative to the emphasis it receives at other universities) tend also to be those universities where academic freedom is valued as a goal; this fact suggests that protection of academic freedom is part of the image of the university. Thus persons who value academic freedom will be attracted to the university or, once there, will tend to remain, whereas persons who put less value on academic freedom will either not be attracted to the university or will tend to leave it and seek employment elsewhere.

As was true with the over-all ratings, output goals involving students are not regarded as particularly meaningful; rather, research and direct service goals are emphasized. In other words, our respondents feel no particular discomfort at being in a university where the emphasis given to student goals is greater or smaller than what they think it should be.

Of the support goals, those involving adaptation and motivation are prominent. The high goal congruence found for the goal of educating to the utmost all legally qualified high school graduates suggests that a university's admissions policy—selective *vs.*

TABLE 2

CONGRUENCE BETWEEN PERCEIVED AND PREFERRED GOALS: ACROSS UNIVERSITIES

Goal	Degree of Congruence [a]
OUTPUT GOALS:	
Student-Expressive	
4–Develop student's objectivity	.731
Student-Instrumental	
6–Prepare students for useful careers	.855
9–Cultivate student's taste	.792
Research	
11–Carry on pure research	.877
12–Carry on applied research	.744
Direct Service	
13–Provide special adult training	.789
14–Assist citizens through extension programs	.941
16–Disseminate new ideas	.569
17–Preserve cultural heritage	.664
SUPPORT GOALS:	
Adaptation	
18–Ensure confidence of contributors	.562
19–Ensure favor of validating bodies	.530
20–Educate to utmost high school graduates	.970
22–Satisfy area needs	.898
23–Keep costs down	.535
Management	
26–Involve faculty in university government	.466
27–Involve students in university government	.679
29–Keep harmony	.481
31–Emphasize undergraduate instruction	.703
Motivation	
35–Protect academic freedom	.883
36–Give faculty maximum opportunity to pursue careers	.773
37–Provide student activities	.533
38–Protect students' right of inquiry	.744
39–Protect students' right of action	.738
Position	
42–Maintain top quality in all programs	.562
47–Preserve institutional character	.810

[a] Goodman and Kruskal's *gamma*; see Chapter 1, pages 23–24, for explanation.

open-door—is an important determinant of the satisfaction or frustration of the staff member. Should those policies be too inconsistent with what he feels to be "right," he will probably not remain at the institution. The same is true for the goal of satisfying the needs of the immediate geographical region and the related output goal of assisting citizens through extension programs, advice, consultation, and so forth. Taken together with the fact that both research goals—pure and applied—appear in the table, these findings suggest that there is a clear distinction between "service" goals and "elitist" goals and that this distinction is of major importance in recruiting and keeping faculty and staff.[2]

Management and position goals, on the other hand, are subordinated in that discrepancies between the ideal and the actual are regarded as being of little significance. It is interesting to note that the management goals of rewarding people according to their contributions either to their discipline or to the institution do not appear in the table. Apparently, people find it possible to work in universities where rewards are apportioned on a basis of which they disapprove; moreover, the university seems to have room for both the discipline-oriented and the institution-oriented person. The high degree of congruence on the position goal of preserving the character of the institution (which, it will be recalled, ranks very low both as a perceived and as a preferred goal) suggests that people will not remain long in a place where they are in profound disagreement with the emphasis placed on this objective. Interestingly enough, the goal concerned with maintaining or increasing the university's prestige does not appear in the table. Perhaps in those cases in which less effort is being expended on this goal than the individual feels is desirable, his goal preference is an expression of the attachment and fondness that he nonetheless feels for the institution.

[2] As will be shown in subsequent chapters, there is a clear distinction between "elitist" goals and "service" goals. Elitist goals reflect an "ivory tower" orientation: a concern with scholarly and intellectual values at the expense of more practical considerations, with faculty interests, and with prestige and excellence. "Service" goals, on the other hand, are related to a concern with developing other capacities and skills in the student besides just his intellect, with providing direct service to the surrounding community, with satisfying outside constituencies, and with the good of the institution. Looked at another way, "service" goals are those traditionally associated with land-grant institutions. It should be pointed out, however, that universities other than land-grant institutions may manifest such a pattern and that not all land-grant universities necessarily have identical "service" goal structures.

Within-University Analysis

Table 3 shows the statistically significant goal congruences found in the within-university analysis. As in the across-universities analysis, the number of findings is large (21 out of the 47 goals), making it reasonable to infer that at universities where a goal receives great emphasis relative to other goals, the feeling is likely to be that the goal should be emphasized. In three instances—developing the student's intellect, protecting the faculty's academic freedom, and letting the will of the faculty prevail—the correspondence is perfect. For all three, both the perceived and the preferred goal always fall in the top third of the distribution.

TABLE 3

CONGRUENCE BETWEEN PERCEIVED AND PREFERRED GOALS: WITHIN UNIVERSITY

Goal	Degree of Congruence [a]
OUTPUT GOALS:	
Student-Expressive	
1–Cultivate student's intellect	1.000 [b]
2–Produce well-rounded student	.588
3–Affect student with great ideas	.668
Student-Instrumental	
6–Prepare students for useful careers	.941
7–Prepare students for status/leadership	.825
Research	
11–Carry on pure research	.940
Direct Service	
13–Provide special adult training	.732
14–Assist citizens through extension programs	.968
15–Provide community cultural leadership	.676
16–Disseminate new ideas	.898
17–Preserve cultural heritage	.672
SUPPORT GOALS:	
Adaptation	
20–Educate to utmost high school graduates	.743
24–Hold staff in face of inducements	.855
Management	
26–Involve faculty in university government	.756
32–Encourage graduate work	.805
34–Let will of faculty prevail	1.000 [b]
Motivation	
36–Give faculty maximum opportunity to pursue careers	.906
38–Protect students' right of inquiry	.754
39–Protect students' right of action	.857
Position	
44–Maintain balanced quality in all programs	.831

[a] Goodman and Kruskal's *gamma*; see Chapter 1, page 23, for explanation.
[b] Both perceived and preferred goals always fall in top third in all universities.

Within the institution, congruence in output goals seems to be of more significance than congruence in support goals: Only one-third of the total number of support goals appear in the table, compared with close to two-thirds of the output goals. All five relating to direct service are significant. Moreover, goals relating to students are given greater prominence. In general, we may infer that persons find it more important to be in settings where perceived and preferred output goals are congruent than in settings where perceived and preferred support goals are congruent. Since students and other clients judge universities on the basis of their output and since most faculty members are directly involved in output of one sort or another, this finding is to be expected.

Of the support goals, congruence between perception and preference is particularly important for the goals of letting the will of the faculty prevail on all important issues, giving faculty members maximum opportunity to pursue their careers according to their own criteria, protecting the students' right to advocate and practice direct political and social action, holding on to staff in the face of inducements from other universities, maintaining a balanced quality in all programs, and encouraging graduate work. But in view of the comparatively small number of findings for support goals, we can safely conclude that both faculty members and administrators can work in situations where they are not receiving the kind of support that they regard as desirable, as long as the university is producing the graduates, research, and direct services that they think it ought to be producing.

Chapter 3

THE RELATIONSHIP BETWEEN
GOALS AND GLOBAL CHARACTERISTICS

In most studies concerned with academic institutions, it is assumed that such characteristics as size, curricular emphasis, and prestige are closely associated with other more subtle aspects of an institution's atmosphere and orientation. In order to explore more fully the impact of these characteristics, called "global"[1] because they apply to the institution as a whole, we compared the goal emphases of different types of universities. The global measures considered were the following:

1. Size (of full-time staff and of student body)
2. Location (geographical region and urban *vs.* rural location)
3. Type of control (public *vs.* private)
4. Productivity (number of doctorates awarded and volume of contract research)
5. Prestige (Cartter quality rating)[2]
6. Graduate emphasis (proportion of graduate students in the total student body)[3]

Information was derived primarily from *American Universities and Colleges*[4] and applies to the 1962–63 academic year.

The first two of the six global characteristics proved to have little relation to goal structure. Although an academic institution's size is commonly assumed to affect strongly its "climate," and though the rapid growth of our universities is almost universally

---

[1] The term "global" was suggested by the usage in Paul F. Lazarsfeld and Herbert Menzel, "On the Relation Between Individual and Collective Properties," in *Complex Organizations*, ed. Amitai Etzioni (New York: Holt, Rinehart, and Winston, 1961), pp. 428-29.

[2] Allan M. Cartter (ed.), *An Assessment of Quality in Graduate Education* (Washington: American Council on Education, 1966). Cartter's scores have been corrected to allow for differences in the number of departments rated at various universities in his sample. See Appendix B.

[3] The intercorrelations of these global characteristics were low.

[4] Allan M. Cartter (ed.), *American Universities and Colleges*, 9th edition (Washington: American Council on Education, 1964).

decried as erosive of the finest ideals of higher education, it seems that in fact the larger universities work toward essentially the same goals as do the smaller ones. The only findings that emerged were that as the size of the full-time teaching, research, and administrative staff increases, more emphasis is given to doing pure research, disseminating new ideas, and keeping up to date, and lower value is assigned to developing pride in the university; as the size of the student body increases, providing cultural leadership to the community is given slightly more prominence, carrying on applied research is regarded as a worthy goal, and encouraging graduate work is not. These relationships very probably reflect chance factors. The absence of differences cannot be attributed to a lack of variation in the sample, which was fairly heterogeneous: About 30 of the 68 universities had student bodies of 15,000 or over, and the smallest had about 3,000.

A university's geographical location has almost no bearing on its perceived or preferred goal structures, except that universities in the East South Central and the Pacific regions seem to give more emphasis to involving students in university government than do universities in other regions. The analyses of the differences between universities located in rural areas and those located in urban areas were more fruitful. Rural universities tend to give relatively great attention to assisting citizens through extension services, involving students in university government, and providing a full round of student activities—goals which seem appropriate, considering the rural university's relative isolation and closer ties with a farming community. Urban universities tend to emphasize maintaining or increasing prestige.

Differences in the structure of preferred goals, particularly output goals, are more marked (see *Table 4*). At universities located in rural areas, the preference is for the practical goals associated with the "service" orientation, whereas at universities in urban areas, the preference is for the elitist goals associated with the scholarly orientation. For instance, persons at rural universities do not place a high value on developing the student's objectivity and training him for scholarship and research (as persons at urban universities do), but rather favor preparing him for a useful career, making an effective citizen of him, and aiding him in upward mobility. That the protection of students' rights to advocate and take part in political and social action should be regarded more highly at urban than at rural universities is not surprising. It is probable that students in metropolitan areas are more likely to be politically aware and active and that faculty and administrators, with their strong commitment to the exercise of freedom, are more accepting of these tendencies than are their rural counterparts.

These findings, though interesting, are meager compared with the findings that emerged from the analyses for type of control, productivity, prestige, and graduate emphasis. These are discussed in the remainder of the chapter, which is divided into two major sections, the first dealing with the relation between global characteristics and perceived goals, and the second with the relation between global characteristics and preferred goals. To make comparison easier, *Table 4* through *Table 10* show the statistically

TABLE 4

THE RELATIONSHIP BETWEEN LOCATION (URBAN *vs.* RURAL) AND PREFERRED UNIVERSITY GOALS

Goal	Across Universities	Within University
OUTPUT GOALS:		
Student-Expressive		
4–Develop student's objectivity.............	−.735	——
Student-Instrumental		
6–Prepare students for useful careers........	.571	.750
7–Prepare students for status/leadership....	.531	——
8–Train students for scholarship/research....	−.571	——
10–Prepare student for citizenship...........	——	.922
Research		
12–Carry on applied research...............	——	.650
Direct Service		
13–Provide special adult training............	.542	——
14–Assist citizens through extension programs	.636	.698
17–Preserve cultural heritage...............	——	−.810
SUPPORT GOALS:		
Adaptation		
20–Educate to utmost high school graduates...	.579	——
21–Accept good students only...............	−.740	−.875
Motivation		
35–Protect academic freedom...............	−.623	——
37–Provide student activities...............	.578	——
39–Protect students' right of action..........	−.568	——
Position		
45–Keep up to date........................	.620	——

NOTE.—Positive *gamma* indicates that the goal is valued highly at rural universities. Negative *gamma* indicates that it is valued highly at urban universities.

significant correlations for both perceived and preferred goals side by side. Unless otherwise noted, all tables should be read as follows: The goals listed in each table are those which significantly differentiate universities ranking high on the criterion from those ranking low. A positive *gamma* signifies that the goal tends to be important (in the sense of its either being emphasized or being valued, depending on whether the perceived or the preferred goal analysis is involved) at the high-ranking universities and to be relatively unimportant at the low-ranking universities. Conversely, a negative *gamma* means that the goal is given prominence at the low-ranking universities but downgraded at the high-ranking ones.

PERCEIVED GOALS AND GLOBAL CHARACTERISTICS

How do universities of different types differ in their goal emphases? To answer this question, the two kinds of analyses mentioned in the previous chapter were again used: across universities, in which universities were compared with respect to their mean scores on a particular perceived goal, and within university, in which universities were compared with respect to the rank which they gave a particular goal relative to other goals at the same university. It should be remembered that we are examining the perceptions of faculty members and administrators at the institution, with what they observe and report to be the actual goals of the institution. Moreover, we have not concerned ourselves with success in attaining the goals pursued.

Type of Control

Of the global characteristics considered, type of control proved to be one of the most significant in accounting for differences in the goal emphases of different institutions. Apparently public universities work toward different goals than do private universities.[5] The results of the analyses for type of control are shown in *Table 5* and *Table 6*. The goals that had positive relationships in the analyses for private universities had negative relationships in the analyses for public universities, and vice versa, so the two tables should be examined together for a better understanding of the full picture.

---

[5] The private universities considered in these analyses were all nonsectarian. It is conceivable that church-related universities have still other sets of goals.

Both the across-universities and within-university analyses revealed significant differences in the output goals of public and private universities, particularly with respect to student-expressive goals. Private institutions concern themselves with cultivating the student's intellect, making sure that he is affected permanently by great ideas, and developing his objectivity about himself and his beliefs. In public universities, on the other hand, no student-expressive goals receive particular emphasis. With respect to student-instrumental goals, private universities stress providing students with skills, attitudes, contacts, and experiences which maximize the likelihood of their achieving high status and a position of leadership, and training them in the methods of scholarship and research, whereas public universities stress preparing students for useful careers. That the private university should tend to give a higher rank, relative to other goals, to the "upward mobility" goal may seem somewhat surprising, since many people think of the state university as the place where children from less affluent families go to acquire the training they need to improve their social status. Perhaps the state university sees its mission as being to give the student the educational background —and the academic degree—that will permit him to move up the status scale occupationally, whereas the private university sees itself as providing not only the professional skills but also the cultural background and polish necessary for upward mobility.

Differences in the research and direct service goals of the two types of institution seem to reflect a distinction between fulfilling immediate needs and serving more abstract but less practical ends: State universities give priority to carrying on applied research, assisting citizens through extension programs and similar services, and providing cultural leadership to the community through programs in the arts, public lectures, exhibits, and so forth. Private universities give greater (though not significantly so) emphasis to doing pure research and see themselves as centers for the dissemination of new ideas.

State and private universities differ in the patterning of their support goals too. The adaptation goals that receive emphasis at the two types of institution are consistent with the research and service goals. Their admissions policies are diametrically opposed: Private universities are more interested in students of high potential, whereas public universities concern themselves with educating all high school graduates who meet the legal requirements for admission. Moreover, the public universities emphasize satisfying the needs and solving the problems of the immediate geographical region—a goal closely connected to the direct service goal of providing extension services—and keeping costs as low as possible, no doubt to satisfy the legislative committees which con-

TABLE 5

THE RELATIONSHIP BETWEEN TYPE OF CONTROL AND UNIVERSITY GOALS
(Private Universities)

GOALS	PERCEIVED GOALS		PREFERRED GOALS	
	1	2	1	2
OUTPUT GOALS:				
Student-Expressive				
1–Cultivate student's intellect..	.788	.862	—	—
3–Affect student with great ideas....................	.784	.848	—	.585
4–Develop student's objectivity.....................	.741	.931	.773	—
Student-Instrumental				
7–Prepare students for status/ leadership...............	—	.563	—	—
8–Train students for scholarship/research............	.599	—	.525	—
Direct Service				
16–Disseminate new ideas......	.531	.535	—	—
17–Preserve cultural heritage....	—	—	—	.736
SUPPORT GOALS:				
Adaptation				
18–Ensure confidence of contributors.....................	.548	—	—	—
21–Accept good students only...	.874	.888	.924	.935
Management				
32–Encourage graduate work....	.602	—	—	.746
Motivation				
35–Protect academic freedom....	.627	—	.698	—
36–Give faculty maximum opportunity to pursue careers.	.535	.604	.675	.729
38–Protect students' right of inquiry...................	.566	—	—	—
39–Protect students' right of action.....................	—	—	—	.714
Position				
42–Maintain top quality in all programs...............	—	—	.814	—
45–Keep up to date...........	.552	—	—	—
46–Increase or maintain prestige.	.647	—	—	—
47–Preserve institutional character....................	.573	—	.724	—

1 = across-universities goals analysis   2 = within-university goals analysis

NOTE.—For the goals that are negatively related to private control, see Table 6.

trol their budgets. In addition, they give high priority (relative to other goals) to ensuring the favorable appraisal of validating bodies (e.g., accrediting agencies, professional societies) and to restraining their staff from yielding to lures and inducements from other universities. Private universities, being more depen-

TABLE 6

THE RELATIONSHIP BETWEEN TYPE OF CONTROL AND UNIVERSITY GOALS
(State Universities)

GOALS	PERCEIVED GOALS		PREFERRED GOALS	
	1	2	1	2
OUTPUT GOALS:				
Student-Expressive				
2–Produce well-rounded student	—	—	.658	.637
Student-Instrumental				
6–Prepare students for useful careers	.603	.673	.675	.613
9–Cultivate student's taste	—	—	.626	—
10–Prepare student for citizenship	—	—	.627	.716
Research				
12–Carry on applied research	.552	.705	.718	.604
Direct Service				
13–Provide special adult training	—	—	.780	—
14–Assist citizens through extension programs	.837	.767	.861	.916
15–Provide community cultural leadership	—	.569	.501	—
SUPPORT GOALS				
Adaptation				
19–Ensure favor of validating bodies	—	.680	.511	—
20–Educate to utmost high school graduates	.941	.844	.924	.930
22–Satisfy area needs	.718	.533	.668	—
23–Keep costs down	.626	.562	—	—
24–Hold staff in face of inducements	—	.593	.697	.599
Management				
25–Reward for contribution to profession	—	—	.564	—
27–Involve students in university government	.801	—	.553	—
29–Keep harmony	.688	—	—	—
31–Emphasize undergraduate instruction	.599	—	—	—
Motivation				
37–Provide student activities	.602	.638	—	—

1 = across-universities goals analysis   2 = within-university goals analysis

NOTE.—For the goals that are negatively related to public control, see Table 5.

dent on nongovernment funds, are more inclined to emphasize the goal of ensuring the confidence and support of their private financial contributors.

The two types of institution also differ in their management goals, particularly in those relating to graduate work. Private universities give a high rating to encouraging students to go into graduate work, and public universities are more inclined to devote attention to undergraduate instruction even at the cost of the graduate program. In addition, public institutions tend to give greater emphasis to involving students in the government of the university and to keeping harmony among various departments and divisions in the university.

Private universities are perceived as being more concerned than are state universities with the protection of the faculty's academic freedom. It should be borne in mind, however, that all the institutions in our sample gave this goal high priority. It ranked in the top third of the distribution of goals at 41 of the 42 state universities and at all 26 private universities. When universities are ranged in order of their mean scores on this goal, however, private universities are more likely to be found in the top third of the distribution. In addition, private universities emphasize the goals of giving the faculty member maximum opportunity to pursue his career in a manner most satisfactory to him and of protecting the student's right to inquire and investigate, while public institutions emphasize providing a full round of student activities.

None of the position goals receive significantly heavier emphasis at public universities, but at private universities, the goals of keeping up to date, maintaining or increasing the institution's prestige, and preserving its distinctive character are important. These relationships may reflect the elitist orientation and the individualistic nature of the private institution. Since the public university is more caught up in the push and pull of everyday affairs, it may have less opportunity to devote attention to these matters.

Those goals which receive equal emphasis in both public and private universities deserve mention. For example, the two types of institution do not differ markedly in their attention (or lack of it) to the output goals of producing a student who is well-rounded, morally sound, judicious in his tastes, and effective as a citizen. Although state universities are likely to stress involving students in university government (a goal which, in any case, is ranked low at almost all institutions; see *Table 1*, page 28), other goals relating to university governance are not associated with one type of institution or the other. Moreover, in spite of the relatively greater emphasis which the private university places on maintaining its own particular character, it does not stress to a greater extent than does the state university the development of loyalty to or greater pride in the institution.

One rather striking difference between the across-universities and the within-university analyses is that the former produced a number of significant findings for support goals, whereas the latter produced comparatively few, and most of those were in the adaptation category. This difference may mean that public and private universities do not diverge markedly in the relative priority they give to most support goals within the university's overall structure. The most pronounced differences are that private universities tend to have higher mean scores on certain support goals in the motivation and position categories (though they are no more likely to rank these goals above others within the institution) and that state universities tend to give high priority over other goals to adaptation goals which involve satisfying constituencies outside the university (winning the favorable appraisal of validating bodies, keeping costs down, and satisfying local area needs).

Productivity

A university's productivity was assessed in two ways: by the number of doctorates it awarded in the academic year 1962–63 and by its dollar volume of contract research. Though these indices reflect different types of output, and probably a different set of influences, both are meaningful measures of productivity, and both are closely related to goals associated with graduate work and research, activities central to universities.

As *Table 7* indicates, universities in the top third in doctorate production give strong emphasis to the output goals of training students in methods of scholarship, doing pure research, and disseminating new ideas. Moreover, they tend to have high mean scores on the goals of seeing to it that the student is permanently affected by great ideas, developing his objectivity, and preserving the cultural heritage. Universities which award relatively few doctorates, on the other hand, tend to give higher priority to producing students who can perform their citizenship duties effectively and to preparing them specifically for useful careers.

With respect to support goals, the high and low productivity groups are differentiated in the attention they give to allowing the professor maximum opportunity to pursue his career as he sees fit (a goal emphasized by the high doctorate producers) and to ensuring the favorable appraisal of validating bodies (a goal emphasized by the low doctorate producers). Moreover, the more productive institutions tend to have high mean scores on the goals of encouraging students to go into graduate work, rewarding faculty members for their contribution to their profession or discipline (rather than to the institution), and maintaining top

TABLE 7

The Relationship Between Productivity, As Measured by Number of Doctorates Awarded, 1962–63, and University Goals

GOALS	PERCEIVED GOALS		PREFERRED GOALS	
	1	2	1	2
OUTPUT GOALS:				
Student-Expressive				
3–Affect student with great ideas	.473	——	——	——
4–Develop student's objectivity	.479	——	——	——
Student-Instrumental				
6–Prepare students for useful careers	——	−.577	−.476	——
8–Train students for scholarship/research	.690	.810	——	——
10–Prepare students for citizenship	——	−.651	——	——
Research				
11–Carry on pure research	.685	.686	.571	.579
Direct Service				
15–Provide community cultural leadership	——	——	−.459	——
16–Disseminate new ideas	.608	.684	——	——
17–Preserve cultural heritage	.478	——	——	——
SUPPORT GOALS:				
Adaptation				
19–Ensure favor of validating bodies	−.519	−.865	−.509	−.542
21–Accept good students only	——	.510	——	——
22–Satisfy area needs	——	−.525	−.534	——
Management				
25–Reward for contribution to profession	.602	——	——	——

quality in all or some programs, keeping up to date, and increasing or maintaining prestige. None of these goals, however, appeared in the results for the within-university analysis; thus, the top doctorate producers are no more inclined than are the low doctorate producers to rank these goals high relative to other goals within the same institution. To put it another way, they do not sacrifice output goals to support goals—in particular, to position goals relating to their status vis-a-vis other universities. They do tend, however, to give a significantly higher rank to the goal of accommodating only students of high potential.

The less productive institutions, on the other hand, tend to have higher mean scores on emphasizing undergraduate instruc-

TABLE 7 *continued*

GOALS	PERCEIVED GOALS		PREFERRED GOALS	
	1	2	1	2
SUPPORT GOALS: *continued*				
26–Involve faculty in university government.............	——	——	——	.648
29–Keep harmony............	——	——	−.473	——
30–Reward for contribution to institution..............	——	——	——	−.758
31–Emphasize undergraduate instruction...............	−.575	——	−.463	——
32–Encourage graduate work....	.641	——	——	——
33–Ensure efficient goal attainment....................	——	——	−.618	——
Motivation				
36–Give faculty maximum opportunity to pursue careers.	.456	.458	——	——
38–Protect students' right of inquiry.................	——	——	——	.665
39–Protect students' right of action..................	——	——	——	.908
40–Develop faculty loyalty to institution..............	——	——	−.535	——
41–Develop pride in university..	——	——	−.654	−.814
Position				
42–Maintain top quality in all programs................	.528	——	——	——
43–Maintain top quality in important programs.........	.630	——	——	——
45–Keep up to date............	.719	——	——	——
46–Increase or maintain prestige	.446	——	——	——

1 = across-universities goals analysis   2 = within-university goals analysis

tion and to give higher priority to satisfying the needs of the local geographical area.

The pattern of perceived goals associated with dollar volume of contract research is essentially the same (see *Table 8*), although the number of goals that differentiate the highly productive universities from the less productive on this measure is greater. Universities that carry out a large amount of contract research do not place particular emphasis on preserving the cultural heritage, as do the universities that award a large number of doctoral degrees; rather, they stress developing the student's intellect, preserving the faculty's academic freedom, and protecting the

TABLE 8

THE RELATIONSHIP BETWEEN PRODUCTIVITY, AS MEASURED BY VOLUME OF CONTRACT RESEARCH, AND UNIVERSITY GOALS

GOALS	PERCEIVED GOALS		PREFERRED GOALS	
	1	2	1	2
OUTPUT GOALS:				
Student-Expressive				
1–Cultivate student's intellect..	.587	——	——	——
2–Produce well-rounded student	——	——	−.557	−.571
3–Affect student with great ideas....................	.508	——	——	——
4–Develop student's objectivity	.573	——	——	——
5–Develop student's character..	——	——	——	−.578
Student-Instrumental				
6–Prepare students for useful careers.................	−.479	−.510	−.561	——
8–Train students for scholarship/research............	.694	.718	——	——
9–Cultivate student's taste....	−.606	——	−.497	——
10–Prepare student for citizenship...................	——	−.533	−.453	——
Research				
11–Carry on pure research......	.773	.699	.665	.795
Direct Service				
14–Assist citizens through extension programs...........	——	−.521	−.480	——
15–Provide community cultural leadership.............	——	——	−.511	——
16–Disseminate new ideas......	.695	.752	——	——
SUPPORT GOALS:				
Adaptation				
19–Ensure favor of validating bodies...................	——	−.754	−.453	——
20–Educate to utmost high school graduates.........	——	−.476	−.451	——
21–Accept good students only...	.634	.639	.556	.667
22–Satisfy area needs..........	−.556	−.552	−.455	——
23–Keep costs down...........	——	−.476	——	——

student's right of inquiry—goals that receive no particular emphasis at the high doctorate producers.

Many of the goals that proved significant in the analyses for contract research but not in those for doctorate production had negative correlations, indicating that they are given high priority at universities that do relatively little contract research but are subordinated at universities that do a great deal. These goals include cultivating the student's taste, assisting citizens, accommodating all legally qualified high school graduates, keeping costs down, giving students a voice in university government, keeping harmony among divisions of the university, and providing student

TABLE 8 *continued*

GOALS	PERCEIVED GOALS		PREFERRED GOALS	
	1	2	1	2
SUPPORT GOALS: *continued*				
24–Hold staff in face of inducements	——	——	——	−.501
Management				
25–Reward for contribution to profession	.632	.531	——	——
26–Involve faculty in university government	——	——	——	.702
27–Involve students in university government	−.499	——	——	——
29–Keep harmony	−.496	——	——	——
30–Reward for contribution to institution	——	——	——	−.645
31–Emphasize undergraduate instruction	−.680	——	−.494	——
32–Encourage graduate work	.687	.575	——	——
33–Ensure efficient goal attainment	——	——	−.537	——
Motivation				
35–Protect academic freedom	.466	——	.533	——
36–Give faculty maximum opportunity to pursue careers	.561	.621	——	——
37–Provide student activities	——	−.554	——	——
38–Protect students' right of inquiry	.503	——	——	——
41–Develop pride in university	——	——	−.472	——
Position				
42–Maintain top quality in all programs	.706	.833	——	——
43–Maintain top quality in important programs	.643	——	——	——
45–Keep up to date	.802	——	——	——
46–Increase or maintain prestige	.604	——	——	——

1 = across-universities goals analysis   2 = within-university goals analysis

activities. These additional findings are consistent with the conclusion that at the most highly productive institutions, with respect both to doctorate production and to contract research, energy is devoted primarily to scholarly and professional goals at the expense of more limited local and practical goals.

Prestige

Originally, two measures intended to assess an institution's quality were used: a corrected version of Cartter's quality scores (see *Appendix B,* page 128) and—much cruder, but easily accessible—number of volumes in the library. Though one might off-

TABLE 9

THE RELATIONSHIP BETWEEN PRESTIGE AND UNIVERSITY GOALS

GOALS	PERCEIVED GOALS		PREFERRED GOALS	
	1	2	1	2
OUTPUT GOALS:				
Student-Expressive				
1–Cultivate student's intellect..	.516	—	—	—
2–Produce well-rounded student....................	—	—	−.639	−.784
3–Affect student with great ideas....................	.473	—	—	—
4–Develop student's objectivity.	.703	—	—	—
5–Develop student's character..	—	—	−.547	−.559
Student-Instrumental				
6–Prepare students for useful careers..................	−.504	−.792	−.598	−.619
8–Train students for scholarship/research............	.730	.740	—	—
9–Cultivate student's taste.....	−.553	—	−.569	—
10–Prepare students for citizenship....................	—	−.541	−.463	—
Research				
11–Carry on pure research......	.891	.887	.734	.684
Direct Service				
13–Provide special adult training.....................	—	—	−.453	—
14–Assist citizens through extension programs............	−.455	−.619	−.526	−.620
15–Provide community cultural leadership..............	—	—	−.461	—
16–Disseminate new ideas.......	.799	.822	.455	—
17–Preserve cultural heritage....	.651	.541	—	.507
SUPPORT GOALS:				
Adaptation				
19–Ensure favor of validating bodies...................	−.583	−.914	−.580	−.580
20–Educate to utmost high school graduates..........	—	−.472	−.463	—

hand suppose that a university's library holdings are more a function of its size than of any other characteristic, such is not the case; Cartter found a very close correlation (coefficient = .79) between an institution's quality rating and the size of its library holdings. Our analyses gave strong confirmation to this finding: The lists of the goals significantly related to number of volumes in the library and to prestige were practically identical. Therefore, to avoid redundancy, we report only the relationships between prestige and goals.

The number of significant relationships revealed in both the across-universities and within-university analyses was considerable (see *Table 9*). Apparently a university's prestige—the popu-

TABLE 9 *continued*

GOALS	PERCEIVED GOALS		PREFERRED GOALS	
	1	2	1	2
SUPPORT GOALS: *continued*				
21–Accept good students only...	.556	.666	.521	.725
22–Satisfy area needs..........	−.628	−.686	−.603	——
23–Keep costs down...........	−.448	−.457	−.531	——
Management				
25–Reward for contribution to profession...............	.772	.703	——	——
26–Involve faculty in university government..........	——	——	——	.751
29–Keep harmony...........	——	——	−.598	——
30–Reward for contribution to institution..............	——	——	−.519	−.792
31–Emphasize undergraduate instruction................	−.697	——	−.549	——
32–Encourage graduate work....	.709	——	——	——
33–Ensure efficient goal attainment..................	——	——	−.575	——
34–Let will of faculty prevail....	——	.507	——	.769
Motivation				
35–Protect academic freedom...	.496	——	.543	——
36–Give faculty maximum opportunity to pursue careers	.657	.648	.521	.555
38–Protect students' right of inquiry.................	.517	——	——	.895
39–Protect students' right of action..................	——	——	——	.951
41–Develop pride in university...	——	——	−.578	−.825
Position				
42–Maintain top quality in all programs...............	.705	.552	——	——
43–Maintain top quality in important programs.........	.756	——	——	——
45–Keep up to date...........	.818	——	——	——
46–Increase or maintain prestige...................	.691	——	——	——

1 = across-universities goals analysis   2 = within-university goals analysis

lar image of its quality—is one of its most distinctive features, and this distinction may well differentiate the university from other types of organization. To put it another way, universities seem to have definite "quality" labels attached to them; they are regarded as "outstanding," as "above average," or as "mediocre." To determine the validity of these labels as indications of the institution's actual quality—whether judged by the character and success of its graduates or by its contributions to knowledge and to the needs of society or whatever—is another, much more complicated, and perhaps unanswerable question. Suffice it to say that this label does bear a close relationship to its perceived goal structure.

Among the goals that receive great emphasis at the most prestigious universities (that is, those ranking in the top third) but little emphasis at the least prestigious are many which have appeared together before, in the analyses by type of control and productivity. Like private universities and highly productive universities, the "best" universities give precedence to the goals of developing the student's skills in scholarship and research, doing pure research, disseminating new ideas, preserving the cultural heritage, rewarding faculty members for their contributions to their profession, encouraging students to go into graduate work, giving professors maximum opportunity to pursue their careers, and maintaining top quality in all programs.

With regard to their attitudes toward students, the most prestigious universities, not surprisingly, seek to be more selective in their admissions policies. Moreover, in addition to attempting to develop the student's scholarly skills, they give higher ratings than do nonprestigious institutions to the three student-expressive goals that may be described as "intellective": developing the student's intellect, making sure that he is permanently affected by great ideas, and developing his objectivity and critical ability. On the other hand, within the institution, these goals are not ranked particularly high relative to other goals. There are no differences among universities of different prestige levels in the emphasis given to the other two student-expressive goals: producing a well-rounded student (that is, a student who has had all his human potentialities, not just the intellectual or scholarly ones, cultivated) and developing character so that the student can make sound moral choices. The implication here is that if parents are primarily interested in having their child's intellect cultivated, they should send him to one of the more prestigious universities. If they are more concerned with finding an institution which will seek to develop a student's moral character and full human potentialities, they stand as good a chance with a prestigious university as with a mediocre one. In short, the prestigious universities come out ahead in this comparison.

Insofar as student-instrumental goals are concerned, it is the less prestigious university which is more inclined to stress preparing the student specifically for a useful career, making a discerning consumer of him, and endowing him with the capacities to be a good citizen. At first glance, these findings may seem odd. Why, for example, the negative relationship between high prestige and interest in preparing the student for a useful career? It seems most unlikely that a university could attain a reputation for quality by turning out cultured drones. Three points may help to explain this finding. First, the most prestigious universities do emphasize the instrumental goal of developing the student's skills in scholarship and research. In other words, the careers they emphasize are of a special and high-level nature. Second (and this point is related to the first), the use of the words "specifically" and "useful" in the goal item may imply a rather narrow kind of vocational training, preparation for occupations requiring specific sets of skills rather than broadly creative approaches. Third, the high-prestige university, being more selective, does not have to worry about the future careers of its graduates; since they have more ability or come from advantaged families, they are more likely to be successful and productive. One might also surmise that faculty and administrators at the most prestigious universities give little emphasis to making a good citizen or a discerning consumer of the student because they feel that these matters are simply not the business of an academic institution; they are better attended to by other social institutions like the family.

The more prestigious universities manifest a similar lack of concern about satisfying some kind of constituency: assisting citizens through extension services, solving the problems of the local geographical region, keeping costs down, and ensuring the favorable appraisal of validating groups are all perceived as having little importance. Conversely, less prestigious universities concern themselves more with these goals.

Similarly, undergraduate instruction receives little emphasis at the top universities, a finding that may seem inconsistent with the relatively great attention paid to the goals related to developing the student's mind. Perhaps we can infer here that at such institutions, the primary focus is on the graduate student and that the undergraduate's intellectual abilities are thought to be cultivated not so much through classroom instruction as through exposure to outstanding professors devoted to the values of scholarship and research and through independent study.

Devotion to the pursuit of academic freedom—both for the faculty member and for the student—is another characteristic that distinguishes the highly prestigious university from the less prestigious. Moreover, letting the will of the faculty prevail on all important matters of university government is ranked high relative to other goals at the prestigious university. This analysis was one of the few in which that particular goal proved to be statistically significant. In view of the high priority given to other goals relating to the faculty, we may infer that the top-ranking institutions manifest considerable concern over the well-being and satisfaction of the professor. This inference may, in turn, provide a clue as to why such universities are prestigious. Given these favorable working conditions, such universities will almost certainly attract men and women who are or who promise to be highly productive in their professions and hence acquire a strong reputation. The presence of these highly visible scholars may then lead faculty members and administrators at other institutions to regard the particular university as being of high quality. Since Cartter's quality scores were based on the judgments of a national sample of faculty members and administrators, this interpretation is plausible.

Finally, mention should be made of the emphasis which the prestigious university places on certain position goals. Maintaining top quality in some or all of the institution's programs, keeping up to date, and maintaining or increasing the university's prestige are all rated high in the across-institutions analysis, although they do not necessarily outrank other goals within the university. Apparently, persons at the "best" universities are not only conscious of their institution's status, but also feel that it must be worked at all the time.

Graduate Emphasis

Emphasis on graduate work is a characteristic that differentiates the university from other institutions of higher education.

In this respect, our sample could be described as one in which graduate work is emphasized throughout. It does not follow, however, that all 68 universities emphasize graduate work equally. In order to discover whether comparative graduate emphasis is related to the perceived goal structure of the institution, we calculated the proportion of graduate students in its total enrollment and, again, divided institutions into high, medium, and low groups. Percentage of graduate students was used because it is a simple and readily accessible measure and because it seems logically related to the characteristic being investigated.

The most noteworthy finding to emerge from these analyses was that universities with a large proportion of graduate students emphasize virtually the same goals as do the most prestigious institutions, whereas universities with a smaller proportion have essentially the same goal structures as do the less prestigious ones (see *Table 10*). Like the most prestigious, the most graduate-oriented universities tend to emphasize the output goals of developing the student's intellect, affecting him with great ideas, developing his objectivity, and training him in the methods of scholarship and research; they also devote attention to carrying on pure research, disseminating new ideas, and preserving the cultural heritage. The instrumental goals of preparing the student specifically for a useful career and developing his taste as a consumer are rated low at both the most prestigious and the most graduate-oriented universities. Conversely, universities ranking low on these criteria give these goals a relatively higher rating. (Again, it should be remembered that the second of these goals is at the very bottom of the list of perceived goals [see *Table 2*, page 39]; rarely is it rated as being of great or top importance at any university.)

The pattern of support goals is also similar for the two criteria. Both of the top groups are highly selective in their admissions policies and neither gives much attention to satisfying area needs or keeping costs down. Students are encouraged to do graduate work, undergraduate teaching is somewhat slighted, and professors are rewarded for their contributions to their professions, although these tendencies are less marked at the more graduate-oriented institutions than at more prestigious ones. They have an equal tendency to emphasize letting the will of the faculty prevail on all important issues and allowing faculty members maximum opportunity to pursue their own careers. The more graduate-oriented universities have a slight tendency to give greater emphasis to protecting the faculty's academic freedom and the students' right to inquire. In general, universities with the heaviest emphasis on graduate work seem to give attention to goals relating to the professor's freedom and satisfaction; thus, they are more attractive places to work from the faculty member's point of view.

The same position goals are emphasized by both top-ranked groups, though the tendency to emphasize the goals of maintaining top quality in some or all programs and of keeping up to date is somewhat stronger at the more prestigious institutions.

TABLE 10

THE RELATIONSHIP BETWEEN GRADUATE EMPHASIS AND UNIVERSITY GOALS

GOALS	PERCEIVED GOALS		PREFERRED GOALS	
	1	2	1	2
OUTPUT GOALS:				
Student-Expressive				
1–Cultivate student's intellect..	.614	—	—	—
2–Produce well-rounded student....................	—	—	−.597	−.792
3–Affect student with great ideas...................	.600	—	—	.564
4–Develop student's objectivity.....................	.756	.648	.544	—
Student-Instrumental				
6–Prepare students for useful careers...................	−.616	−.746	−.649	−.698
7–Prepare students for status/leadership..............	—	—	−.622	—
8–Train students for scholarship/research............	.623	.916	—	—
9–Cultivate student's taste.....	−.523	—	−.596	—
10–Prepare students for citizenship..................	—	—	−.500	—
Research				
11–Carry on pure research......	.474	—	—	—
12–Carry on applied research....	—	−.560	−.446	—
Direct Service				
14–Assist citizens through extension programs............	—	−.597	−.468	−.669
15–Provide community cultural leadership..............	—	−.472	—	−.579
16–Disseminate new ideas.......	.596	.518	.523	—
17–Preserve cultural heritage....	.470	—	—	.658
SUPPORT GOALS:				
Adaptation				
19–Ensure favor of validating bodies..................	—	−.714	—	—
20–Educate to utmost high school graduates..........	−.554	−.578	−.597	—

Indeed, insofar as the across-universities comparisons are concerned, the only goals which are significantly related to graduate emphasis but not to prestige are those of educating every legally qualified high school graduate to his utmost capacity (a goal rated low) and of protecting and facilitating the students' right to advocate and take part in direct action of a political and social nature. This second goal may be regarded as the "action" counterpart of the goal of protecting the students' right of inquiry. Its occurrence here is worth pointing out, because this analysis is one of the few in which it proved to be statistically significant. One may speculate that graduate students, being more

TABLE 10 *continued*

GOALS	PERCEIVED GOALS		PREFERRED GOALS	
	1	2	1	2
SUPPORT GOALS: *continued*				
21–Accept good students only...	.626	.756	.581	.801
22–Satisfy area needs...........	−.628	−.602	−.504	——
23–Keep costs down...........	−.498	−.518	−.481	——
Management				
25–Reward for contribution to profession..............	.491	——	——	——
26–Involve faculty in university government.........	——	——	.446	.631
29–Keep harmony............	——	——	−.444	——
30–Reward for contribution to institution.............	——	——	−.586	−.655
31–Emphasize undergraduate instruction..............	−.591	——	−.445	——
32–Encourage graduate work....	.557	——	——	——
33–Ensure efficient goal attainment..................	——	——	−.460	——
34–Let will of faculty prevail....	——	.565	——	——
Motivation				
35–Protect academic freedom....	.669	——	.634	——
36–Give faculty maximum opportunity to pursue careers	.673	.674	.576	.669
37–Provide student activities....	——	−.545	−.451	——
38–Protect students' right of inquiry..................	.614	.604	.503	——
39–Protect students' right of action....................	.453	——	——	.800
Position				
42-Maintain top quality in all programs..............	.596	——	.529	——
43–Maintain top quality in important programs........	.484	——	——	——
45–Keep up to date...........	.503	——	——	——
46–Increase or maintain prestige...................	.700	——	——	——

1 = across-universities goals analysis   2 = within-university goals analysis

mature and having a closer identification with faculty members, may regard participation in political and social action as one way of exercising the freedom which they feel they should have. (It is worth recalling here that the Berkeley Free Speech movement was said to originate among graduate students.[6]) Moreover, we might surmise that faculty and administrators are more inclined to recognize and seek to protect the rights of graduate students than of undergraduates.

The within-university analysis of the relation of goals to graduate emphasis also reveals a pattern similar to the one found for prestige. One exception is the goal of developing the student's objectivity and thus enabling him to examine his beliefs critically, which receives considerable emphasis relative to other goals at universities with a strong graduate emphasis but not at prestigious universities. Perhaps the development of self-critical ability is regarded as a particularly scholarly virtue and thus one especially appropriate to an institution with a high proportion of graduate students. Another exception is the goal of providing cultural leadership to the community, which tends to rank high at universities where graduate emphasis is comparatively weak but is not significantly related to prestige. Still another exception is that at universities where the proportion of graduate students is small, the goal of applied research ranks high, although there is no tendency for universities with a large proportion of graduate students to rank pure research higher than other goals.

Finally, two motivation goals involving students have relationships to the university's graduate emphasis. Where the proportion of graduate students is great, protecting the students' right of inquiry ranks high relative to other goals, whereas providing students with a full round of activities ranks low. Both findings would seem to reflect the greater maturity of the student body, as well as the narrowing of the graduate student's interests to matters intellectual.

PREFERRED GOALS AND GLOBAL CHARACTERISTICS

In the previous section, we focused on the goals which, according to our respondents, their universities pursue. In this section, we consider the goals which the respondents believe their universities should pursue. The discussion centers on how the institu-

---

[6] See, for instance, Seymour M. Lipset and Sheldon S. Wolin (eds.), *The Berkeley Student Revolt* (Garden City, N.Y.: Anchor Books, 1965), Ch. VI.

tion's global characteristics are related to the goal preferences of its academic and administrative staff and what such relationships may imply about attitudes and values at different kinds of universities.

Type of Control

The last two columns of *Tables 5* and *6* (see pages 48, 49) show the relationships between type of control and preferred goals. Persons at private universities are more likely than are those at public universities to assign high value to elitist goals having to do with the student's intellectual and scholarly capacities. They are little concerned with adaptation and management goals, but they do express a preference for the motivation goals involving the faculty's academic freedom and the students' right of advocacy and action; the position goals of maintaining top quality in all programs and preserving the distinctive character of the institution are also highly valued. The prominence given to this last goal may reflect greater awareness of a distinctive institutional character than exists among persons at state universities and a concomitant devotion to this sense of individuality.[7]

Comparing the lists of perceived and preferred goals, we find no outright conflicts. Most striking is the congruence on the goals of accepting good students only and of giving the faculty maximum opportunity to pursue careers. On the other hand, persons at private universities favor the goals of preserving the cultural heritage, protecting the students' right of action, and maintaining top quality in all programs, but feel that these goals do not necessarily receive proper emphasis at their institutions. They tend to feel relatively neutral about some of the goals that *are* emphasized: cultivating the student's intellect, preparing him to occupy a high status or a position of leadership, disseminating new ideas, ensuring the confidence of contributors, protecting students' right of inquiry, keeping up to date, and increasing or maintaining prestige.

State universities, on the other hand, manifest a preferred goal structure consistent with their service mission. For example, persons at these institutions place a relatively high value on the

[7] If church-related universities had been included in the sample, this tendency would probably be even more pronounced.

output goals of preparing the student specifically for a useful career, carrying on applied research, providing extension and consultation services for local citizens, and acting as a community cultural center—goals which are also emphasized.

Moreover, they tend to feel that emphasis *should* be given, even though it may not be, to the goals of making a good consumer and an effective citizen of the student and providing special training for adults. Producing a well-rounded student—one who has had all his potentialities cultivated—is also highly valued though not particularly emphasized. This preference is consistent with the traditional concept of the state university as one which offers a full round of academic programs, in contrast to the private university, which offers a narrower selection and tends to concentrate on the curricula of a classical education.

Consistent with their concern with output goals of a practical and highly visible nature, state university personnel feel that prominence should be given to the adaptation goals of educating as fully as possible all legally qualified students and satisfying the needs of the local geographical area. Moreover, they feel that the attention paid to ensuring the favorable appraisal of validating groups and to holding staff in the face of inducements from other universities is proper. But they are relatively indifferent to holding costs down, keeping harmony, emphasizing undergraduate instruction, and providing student activities, even though they perceive these goals as being stressed.

They feel also that students should be given some voice in university government and that faculty members should be rewarded for their contributions to their profession or discipline. Neither goal appears in the list of perceived goals, and the second seems somewhat inconsistent with the local orientation of public universities.

The most striking difference between the public and the private university—at least with respect to the statistical significance of the findings—is the attitude of their staffs toward selectivity. Those at private universities say that the institution should accommodate only the best students (*gamma* = .938, within-university analysis), whereas those at public universities say that the institution should do its best to educate all legally qualified high school graduates (*gamma* = .930, within-university analysis). This difference epitomizes other differences in their lists of preferred goals.

Productivity

At universities ranking in the top third on doctorate production, respondents are characterized by a tendency to reject certain goals, particularly those that involve "local" values (see *Table 7,* page 52). Except for a tendency to feel strongly that the university should carry out pure research, they manifest little concern over output goals generally. Indeed, they assign relatively low value to such goals as preparing students for useful careers and providing community cultural leadership. This tendency to downgrade certain output goals—producing a well-rounded student, training him for a career, developing his character, taste, and capacities for effective citizenship, and providing extension services and cultural leadership to the citizens of the local community—is even more pronounced at those universities in the top third on dollar volume of contract research, the other measure of productivity (see *Table 8,* page 54). Persons at these universities, too, value pure research.

There are a few discrepancies between the perceived and the preferred output goals of productive universities, though no actual reversals: That is, in no case is a goal that receives emphasis accorded a low value by respondents at an institution, and vice versa. For instance, persons at highly productive universities seem relatively indifferent to the goals of affecting the student permanently with great ideas, developing his objectivity, and training him for scholarship and research. Even though these goals are actually stressed at the more productive universities, there is no inclination to feel that they necessarily deserve such emphasis, but neither is there an inclination to assign them a low value. On the other hand, persons at less productive universities assign a relatively high value to the goal of providing community cultural leadership but do not feel that the goal is particularly emphasized at their institutions.

Most of the support goals appearing in the analysis are assigned a negative value at the more productive universities, where the attitudes and values of the staff, as reflected in their goal preferences, are cosmopolitan and discipline-oriented rather than local and institution-oriented. Again, essentially the same goals are related to both measures of productivity, the only differences being that persons at the high doctorate producers tend to express a preference for the goals of protecting the students' rights of inquiry and of action (the *gamma* for this latter goal, .908, was the highest in the analysis for this criterion) and to assign a low value to keeping harmony and developing faculty loyalty to the institution, whereas at universities ranking high on the contract research criterion, faculty and administrators definitely favor a selective admissions policy, give a high rating to protecting academic freedom, and tend to rank low the goal of holding staff in the face of inducements from other universities, perhaps because inducements to remain are strong enough to ensure that these universities will suffer few losses.

One goal usually rated low at the more productive universities—that of making sure that the university is run by those selected for their ability to attain its goals in the most efficient manner possible—merits special attention, since these analyses are among the few in which it appeared. Perhaps the low rating reflects a suspicion of "efficiency," a feeling that the word implies a narrow and overly businesslike approach which is threatening to academic and scholarly values.

None of the position goals was related to either doctorate production or volume of contract research, in the analyses of preferred goals, although maintaining top quality in all programs or in those programs considered most important, keeping up to date, and maintaining or increasing the university's prestige were perceived as receiving emphasis at the more productive universities. This discrepancy reflects neutrality, and not an outright antipathy toward those goals.

The two indices of productivity seem to get at slightly different sets of values and attitudes. Volume of contract research has more relationships with goals involving students, in that persons at universities ranked high on the measure place little value on such goals. There is much less variation on these particular goals among institutions at different levels of doctorate production.

In general, however, the two measures produce consistent results. Persons at universities which rank high on either one tend to be research-minded and discipline-oriented, whereas persons at universities ranked low on either measure tend to be service-minded and institution-oriented.

Prestige

The large number of significant findings which emerged from the analyses of the relationships between a university's prestige and the goal preferences of its personnel (see *Table 9,* page 56) would seem to support our earlier suggestion that the quality label is of fundamental importance in distinguishing among institutions of higher education. The prestige level of the university at which a person works is closely associated with his values and preferences with respect to both output and support goals. Moreover, as prestige increases, so do the person's notions of what goals should *not* be emphasized, particularly as regards students.

Persons at the most prestigious institutions place a high value on the goals of doing pure research, accepting only the best students, and providing maximum opportunity for faculty members to pursue their careers in the manner most satisfactory to them; all three are perceived as receiving emphasis too. They feel that the university should serve as a center for disseminating new ideas and that it should protect academic freedom. The goals of preserving the cultural heritage, involving the faculty in university government, and (what might be regarded as a more extreme expression of the same goal) letting the will of the faculty prevail on all important issues are ranked high relative to other preferred goals at the more prestigious universities, as are the goals of protecting the students' rights of inquiry and of direct political action.

On the other hand, the output goals of developing the student's full human potentialities and moral character, of providing him with skills for a useful career, and of making him a discerning consumer and a responsible citizen tend to be devalued. The prestige level of the university bears no relation to preferences with respect to other student output goals, even those involving intellective and scholarly development, which in fact are emphasized. Persons at prestigious institutions tend to feel that it should not be the university's role to provide training to adults through extension courses and other special programs, to assist citizens through extension and consultation services, or to serve as a cultural center for the community.

The adaptation goals of ensuring the favorable appraisal of validating groups, educating all legally qualified students, satisfying the needs of the immediate geographical area, and keeping costs down are considered unimportant by persons at the most prestigious universities, as well as receiving relatively little emphasis.

But there are some discrepancies between perceived and preferred goal structures with respect to management and position goals. For instance, at prestigious universities, low value is assigned to the goals of keeping harmony, seeing to it that the university is run by those who can most efficiently attain its goals, and rewarding professors for their contributions to the institution, but there is no concomitant tendency to slight these goals in actuality. Somewhat oddly, the goal of rewarding professors for their contribution to their disciplines, which *is* emphasized, is not particularly valued. Persons at prestigious universities are no more likely than persons at less prestigious universities to express a preference for the goals of maintaining top quality in all programs or in the most important ones, keeping up to date, or increasing or maintaining prestige, even though these goals receive high ratings in the across-universities analysis of perceived goals. In no instance, however, is there a direct conflict between perception and preference.

Graduate Emphasis

A university's emphasis on graduate work has a number of relationships to the goal preferences of its personnel (see *Table 10,* page 62). As was true of persons at the most prestigious universities, faculty and staff at the most graduate-oriented universities have a number of very definite ideas about what should *not* be emphasized. For instance, they place low value on the student-expressive goal of producing a well-rounded person and the student-instrumental goals of making the student a discerning consumer and a good citizen and of providing him with skills to prepare him for a useful career or to aid him in upward mobility. This last goal was not found to have statistically significant relationships, either positive or negative, in the other analyses of goal preferences, except in the case of rural *vs.* urban location, so it is worth noting that persons at universities which have a large proportion of graduate students have a marked tendency to feel that the university should not concern itself with preparing its students to occupy a high status or a position of leadership and that, conversely, those at universities where the proportion of graduate students is low tend to feel that such a concern is desirable.

At universities with a relatively heavy graduate emphasis, carrying on applied research, assisting local citizens through extension programs and similar services, and providing cultural leadership to the community are felt to have little value.

The number of support goals which respondents at these institutions regard as deserving low priority is fairly large, particularly support goals having to do with adaptation and management. Little value is attached to educating all legally qualified students, satisfying area needs, keeping costs down, maintaining harmony among various departments and divisions, rewarding faculty for their contribution to the institution, emphasizing undergraduate instruction, or ensuring that the university is run by those who can achieve its goals most efficiently. The motivation goal of providing a full round of student activities is ranked low relative to other preferred goals within the university. (It was also ranked low in the analysis of perceived goals). Here again is a reflection of the effects of having a large proportion of graduate students—with their more mature interests and greater devotion to specialized subjects—in the student body.

What goals should be important, according to persons at the more graduate-oriented institutions? Making sure that the student is affected permanently by great ideas and developing his objectivity are assigned high priority, as are the direct service goals of disseminating new ideas and preserving the cultural heritage. Moreover, there is a marked tendency to feel that the university should be selective in its admissions policies.

Persons at these institutions also feel that priority should be given to the support goals of involving the faculty in university government, protecting the academic freedom of the faculty and of the students (both students' rights goals appear among the significant findings), giving professors maximum opportunity to pursue their careers according to their own criteria, and maintaining top quality in all programs.

The findings with respect to this global characteristic are similar to the findings with respect to prestige. In both cases, persons at the universities ranking in the top third on these criteria express a preference for elitist over more down-to-earth practical goals. They manifest considerable concern over the well-being of the faculty but comparatively little concern over the needs of undergraduate students and of the surrounding community.

But the patterns are not identical for the two criteria. The most striking difference is that at universities with a relatively high proportion of graduate students, the goal of carrying on pure research is not accorded as high a value as it is at the most prestigious institutions. The goal of carrying on applied research, however, is downgraded by persons at the most graduate-oriented universities.

Moreover, two of the student-expressive goals relating to intellectual development—fostering objectivity and affecting with great ideas—are regarded as deserving emphasis by those at the most graduate-oriented universities. In contrast, none of the student-expressive goals is highly valued by those at the most prestigious universities.

Finally, maintaining top quality in all programs is rated as meriting attention at the more graduate-oriented universities, one of the few instances in the analyses of goal preferences where a position goal proved to be statistically significant.

SUMMARY AND CONCLUSIONS

Most of the global characteristics considered in this chapter proved to be significantly related to both preferred and perceived goal structures. The exceptions were size—there is little evidence that as the staff or the student body increases, actual goals or goal preferences change—and, to a lesser extent, location, although persons at rural universities tend to have somewhat different goal preferences than persons at metropolitan universities. But type of control, productivity, prestige, and graduate emphasis are characteristics that seem meaningful in making distinctions among universities with respect to their goal emphases and the attitudes and values they represent.

The dominant antithesis running through both sets of analyses was that between what we have dubbed elitist values and "service" values. Private universities and universities ranking high in productivity, prestige, or graduate emphasis tend to resemble one another in their goal patterns. They not only give precedence to but also place a high value on output goals associated with the preservation, expansion, and dissemination of knowledge and with support goals associated with the well-being and satisfaction of the faculty and with professional interests. State universities and universities ranking low in productivity, prestige, or graduate emphasis, on the other hand, tend to emphasize and to place a high value on output goals that are at once less narrow (in that they emphasize matters other than the purely intellectual or scholarly) and at the same time more immediately practical: preparing the student for a useful career and making a discerning consumer and effective citizen of him, carrying on applied research, and serving the immediate community by offering special adult programs, assistance through extension services, and cultural programs. The support goals which receive priority, both as perceived and as preferred goals, are those related to satisfying constituencies outside the university (e.g., accepting all legally qualified students, helping to solve local problems, ensuring the favorable appraisal of validating bodies, and keeping costs down) and to fostering the well-being and integrity of the institution (e.g., keeping harmony, emphasizing undergraduate instruction, rewarding professors for their contribution to the institution, and developing pride in and loyalty to the university).

The patterns of goals on these four criteria (type of control, productivity, prestige, and graduate emphasis) are sufficiently distinct from one another that we may safely infer that the measures get at slightly different factors. Nonetheless, the elitist-cosmopolitan *vs.* the practical-local configuration runs throughout the analyses.

Comparing the results of the two sets of analyses, we find that, in general, they seem congruent. At a university of a type where certain goals are emphasized, faculty and administrators usually place high values on the same goals; in any event, they do not rank them as having very low value. These conclusions are, of course, over general. Conceivably there are a few institutions where actual goals run counter to the goal preferences of the staff. But by and large, the situation seems to be one of harmony between what is and what ought to be.

The over-all congruence underscores again the selectivity process at work in our system of higher education. An institution tends to attract persons who are in sympathy with its goals, insofar as they can judge them before actually being at the institution. Presumably, if he discovers serious discrepancies, the person will leave the institution, although he may remain and mitigate his dissatisfaction either by changing his own goal preferences or by working to change the goal emphases of the institution.

Nonetheless, the correspondence between the two sets of analyses was not perfect. For example, with respect to preferred goals, findings were sparse for criteria of type of control and doctorate production. The implication is that though the goal emphases of public and private universities and of high doctorate producers and low doctorate producers may differ significantly, no such sharp differences exist in the goal preferences of persons working at the institutions.

At those universities whose global characteristics are associated with elitist goal patterns, the student-expressive goals associated with intellectual development (cultivate intellect, affect with great ideas, develop objectivity) and the related student-instrumental goal of training students in methods of research and scholarship tend to be emphasized, but not to be particularly valued as important. The same holds true for certain of the position goals, which proved significant in the analyses of perceived goals, but not in the analyses of preferred goals. It does not follow, however, that these discrepancies indicate a state of tension; persons at these universities have no particular feeling that the emphasis placed on these goals is wrong; rather, they are simply no more inclined to give them a high rating than are persons at other types of institutions.

Finally, there is a marked tendency for persons at institutions with elitist characteristics (private control, high doctorate production, large amount of contract research, high prestige, heavy emphasis on graduate work) to have very strong feelings about what goals should *not* be emphasized. They are more concerned with opposing certain emphases, it would seem, than with supporting other tendencies. We would suggest here, on the basis of our own experience and of interviews with faculty and administrators, that as a university gets "better"—that is, as its prestige increases, as it takes on more contract research, or as the proportion of graduate students in its student body grows larger—its staff becomes more independent. Consequently, they are no longer willing to put up with certain goals which they had previously accepted. They become more decided and insistent about the goals that should *not* be emphasized than about the ones that should be.

CHAPTER 4

POWER STRUCTURE AND PERCEIVED GOALS

In our survey of academic administrators and faculty members, we hoped to learn something about the power structure of universities as well as about their goals. By "power structure" is meant a relatively stable distribution of power among the agencies, groups, and persons involved in higher education. More specifically, our aims were to discover (1) what the power structure of the university is, (2) how that structure is related to the global characteristics discussed in the preceding chapter, and (3) how it is related to the goal structure of the university; the analysis here is limited to *perceived* goals.

Accordingly, the questionnaire included several items designed to identify those who make the big decisions in the university (see Section 2 of the questionnaire, *Appendix C,* page 143). In item 2.1, the respondent was asked to indicate his opinion as to how much influence each of 16 agencies, groups, or persons had in determining the major goals of the university *as a whole.* The power groups considered were: regents or trustees, state legislators, private agencies, Federal government agencies, state government agencies, the university president, the vice-president or provost, the dean of the graduate school, the dean of liberal arts, deans of professional schools as a group, chairmen of departments as a group, faculty, students, parents, citizens of the state, and alumni. Respondents were given five alternatives, scored from 5 ("a great deal of say") to 1 ("no say at all").

THE POWER STRUCTURE
OF AMERICAN UNIVERSITIES

To get an over-all picture of the power structure of American universities, we derived the mean score for each of the potential power-holders; these scores (along with the standard deviation for each) are shown in *Table 11*. There are, of course, variations among universities (though they are not so many or so wide as one might assume), and these will be discussed later in the chapter.

In the table, the potential power-holders are ranked from high to low on the basis of their mean scores. At the top are the president, the regents, and the vice-president, all of whom are perceived as having at least "quite a bit of say" (scores of 4 or above). Ranking at the bottom are students, citizens of the state, and parents.

In general, the standard deviations are low, indicating that, throughout our sample of 68 institutions, there was substantial agreement about the power which each person or group held. In those instances where the standard deviation is large, the explanation lies in the inclusion of both public and private universities in the sample. At state universities, legislators, the Federal government, the state government, and the citizens naturally have more power than they do at private institutions, where large private donors have considerable influence.

That presidents are perceived as having great power—and that there is substantial agreement on this point—is not surprising. The president is the chief executive of his institution and is so perceived by faculty, students, and citizens. Our findings suggest that even weak presidents are regarded as having power, but simply not exercising it.

More startling is the high rating given to the regents. The literature suggests—and the comments that we received from regents in the course of our study support this suggestion—that they themselves feel they do not have much power. Perhaps the discrepancy is between having formal power and using that power. Though the board of regents may have ultimate authority, in most instances they seldom exercise it. Rather, they delegate authority to the president, contenting themselves with handling

TABLE 11

THE OVER-ALL POWER STRUCTURE OF AMERICAN UNIVERSITIES

Power-holder (rank order)	Mean Score	Standard Deviation	Power-holder (rank order)	Mean Score	Standard Deviation
President	4.65	.62	Chairmen	3.19	.93
Regents	4.37	.82	Legislators	2.94	1.37
Vice-President	4.12	.82	Federal Government	2.79	1.06
Deans of Professional			State Government	2.72	1.21
Schools	3.62	.84	Large Private		
Dean of Graduate			Donors	2.69	1.06
School	3.59	.89	Alumni	2.61	.90
Dean of Liberal Arts	3.56	.89	Students	2.37	.82
Faculty	3.31	.97	Citizens of State	2.08	1.02
			Parents	1.91	.87

routine matters at their meetings and with helping to raise money for the operation of the university. Or perhaps their high rank is accounted for by the phrasing of the question: "Who make the *big* decisions?" Regents are responsible for selecting a new president, and although the occasion for so doing arises rarely, nonetheless the decision is undeniably a big one. But that explanation seems inadequate. More likely, it is the aloofness of the group— their distance from the ordinary affairs of the campus [1]—which leads not only faculty but also adminstrators to think of them as having great influence. A similar explanation may be given for the high ranking of the vice-president, who also tends to be a somewhat distant figure. It is likely, too, that he acquires some of the power of the president, by a kind of halo effect.

The view that deans of professional schools are becoming more and more powerful is somewhat substantiated by these ratings (though, as is made clear later in the chapter, they may not be the threatening figures that their detractors make of them). Their power, relative to other deans, is probably the result of their many contacts in the community, their freedom from having to justify themselves to the state and its citizens (since the outputs of their schools are of such obvious value to the community), and the large size of many professional schools, particularly schools of education, agriculture, physical education, and business adminstration. Since our sample is composed of universities, it is to be expected that deans of graduate schools are perceived as having considerable power, but it is somewhat surprising that deans of liberal arts too are so regarded.

The rankings at the lower end of the distribution should do much to allay the fears of those who feel that alumni, students, citizens, and parents have too much influence on decisions. Moreover, those agencies which are the source of funds and which are therefore thought to wield a kind of Machiavellian influence on educational policy—the Federal government and the large private donors—are seen as having, at best, only some say in making the big decisions. The middle position of legislators and of the state government probably results from an averaging of their relatively

[1] Regents of American universities are usually "outsiders," in contrast to the situation in some Canadian and British universities. This contrast is pointed out by Sir James Duff and Robert O. Berdahl in *University Government in Canada,* Report of a Commission Sponsored by the Canadian Association of University Teachers and the Association of Universities and Colleges of Canada (Toronto: University of Toronto Press, 1966).

great influence at public universities with their small influence at private institutions.

Finally, faculty and chairmen occupy a position somewhat higher than that of the outside agencies, with faculty perceived as having slightly greater influence on the big decisions. We may infer here that chairmen tend to be regarded as agents of the faculty and that the supposed hierarchy from deans to chairmen to faculty does not in fact exist.

THE RELATIONSHIP BETWEEN POWER STRUCTURE AND GLOBAL CHARACTERISTICS

Our second major focus in considering the power structure of American universities was on the relationship between that structure and the global characteristics discussed in Chapter 3. For two of these characteristics—size and productivity—findings were almost nonexistent. Briefly, in the larger universities, the students are perceived as having little power; the vice-president, however, has relatively great power, perhaps because the president is usually something of an "outside" man, who spends his time winning the support and favor of the community and of potential donors and thus gives the vice-president greater power within the university community. With respect to productivity (which, it will be recalled, was closely related to goal structure), we find that at universities which do a great deal of contract research, the power of the chairmen and of the alumni is relatively great, but the implications of this finding are not clear.

Type of control is the most important characteristic in determining the power structure of a university, and our findings indicate that it is a mistake to assert that private and public institutions are growing more and more alike. There remain between them significant differences, which are reflected (as the next section indicates) in their goal emphases.

At state universities, legislators and citizens of the state have much more influence than they do at private universities and, to a lesser degree, so do the state government, the Federal government, the regents, and parents.

Among the major power-holders at private universities, on the other hand, are the large private donors. Deans of liberal arts and of professional schools tend to receive high ratings at private universities. Moreover, although students and alumni received low rankings in general, they are more likely to be perceived as having influence on decision making at the private university than at the public one. Apparently, there are no significant differences between private and state universities with respect to the power of the president, vice-president, dean of the graduate school, faculty, and chairmen.

TABLE 12

A COMPARISON OF THE POWER STRUCTURE OF PRIVATE AND OF PUBLIC UNIVERSITIES

PRIVATE			PUBLIC		
Power-holder (rank order)	Mean	Standard Deviation	Power-holder (rank order)	Mean	Standard Deviation
President	4.70	.58	President	4.62	.63
Regents	4.24	.88	Regents	4.41	.78
Vice-President	4.10	.82	Vice-President	4.07	.83
Deans of Professional Schools	3.64	.80	Deans of Professional Schools	3.53	.79
Dean of Liberal Arts	3.57	.83	Dean of Graduate School	3.53	.85
Dean of Graduate School	3.54	.87	Legislators	3.45	1.07
Faculty	3.29	.96	Dean of Liberal Arts	3.43	.83
Chairmen	3.16	.90	Faculty	3.27	.93
Large Private Donors	2.84	1.03	Chairmen	3.13	.87
Alumni	2.53	.84	State Government	2.91	1.02
Federal Government	2.53	.99	Federal Government	2.79	.94
Students	2.25	.69	Alumni	2.57	.80
State Government	1.86	.90	Large Private Donors	2.49	.89
Parents	1.70	.68	Students	2.34	.73
Legislators	1.63	.92	Citizens of State	2.28	.88
Citizens of State	1.43	.63	Parents	1.90	.72

Table 12 shows the rank, mean score, and standard deviation for each group at private and at public universities. Our earlier surmise about why legislators and the state government occupy a middle position in the over-all rank order (*Table 11,* page 76) receives confirmation. Legislators occupy the next-to-the-last position at private universities, but are in sixth position at public universities; the relative power of the state government increases too, though the jump is not quite so dramatic. In these cases, however, the standard deviation is high, indicating that respondents do not agree about what influence these two groups have. This uncertainty exists even at public universities, where one would expect the state government and legislators to be universally perceived as having great power.

Large private donors occupy ninth position at private universities, but again the high standard deviation indicates lack of consensus about their power. Their ranking falls slightly at public universities, though the differences in the means are actually rather small. Otherwise, the rank order is essentially the same for the two types of institution.

Turning to one of our measures of quality—the prestige of the institution—we find that at the more prestigious universities, the vice-president and the departmental chairmen are perceived as having a great deal of say in decision making. The good showing of chairmen may result from the important role they play in freeing faculty for research and other activities that add to the institution's prestige.[2]

Number of volumes in the library (our second measure of quality, not discussed in Chapter 3 because the findings for this characteristic were virtually identical with those for prestige) also proved to be significantly related to the power structure. At universities whose library holdings are large, the power of the dean of liberal arts, chairmen of departments, and faculty members is considerable. This finding probably reflects the scholarly orientation of these three power-holders and of their consequent demands for good library facilities.

The graduate emphasis of a university is also related to its power structure. As the proportion of graduate students increases, so does the rated power of private agencies. The power of legislators and of the state government, on the other hand, tends to decline, at state universities as well as private ones (where, of course, these groups have little power to begin with). Moreover, the faculty tends to have more power, relative to other groups, and citizens of the state, less power. Though it would be hazardous to conclude that legislators and the state government interfere with the growth of graduate schools, it is nonetheless clear that at universities where these groups are strongest, graduate emphasis tends to be slight.

Clear regional differences emerged in these analyses of power structure. To summarize, regents are seen as having little power in those universities in the Mid-Atlantic states and relatively great power in universities in the Southern, West North Central, Mountain, and Pacific Coast states. Vice-presidents tend to have comparatively more power in the Northeast, Mid-Atlantic, and

---

[2] It should be noted that a high proportion of our administrator respondents were departmental chairmen. It is possible that chairmen at the more prestigious universities tend to overestimate their own power.

East North Central states and less in the Southern and Pacific Coast states. Parents, though they have little power over-all, emerge as being somewhat more influential with respect to decision making in the East North Central, West North Central, and Pacific Coast states. With respect to their rankings relative to other groups, private agencies are more powerful in the Northeast, Atlantic, and West North Central states and less powerful in the East North Central and Mountain states. It is not at all clear how these results are to be interpreted, but they probably reflect in part traditional differences in the power held by regents and citizens in Midwestern states, in contrast to the relative autonomy enjoyed by universities on the Eastern Seaboard.

Legislators, the state government, and citizens tend to be perceived as having greater power in universities located in rural areas, whereas private agencies have more power in those located in urban areas, perhaps because the private and more prestigious universities tend to be urban.

Looking back over these findings, one comes away with the feeling that the power structures of different kinds of universities do not differ as much as one might assume. The most significant variable is type of control, and the findings here are the obvious ones: legislators, the state govenment, and citizens have more power at state universities. We may cautiously conclude, then, that the power structure of American universities is remarkably uniform throughout the system.

THE RELATIONSHIP BETWEEN POWER STRUCTURE AND PERCEIVED GOALS

To turn to the main focus of this report, this section deals with the relationship between the power structure and the perceived goals of the institution: that is, the goals which, according to our respondents, are actually emphasized. It should be pointed out that we make no attempt to discuss the relationship between power structure and *preferred* goals. Our pupose was to determine how the power of a particular person or group affects goals. For instance, does the university in which regents have relatively great power pursue different goals than the university in which the faculty has power?

To answer such questions, we used the two types of analyses (across-universities and within-university) for both power structure and goals. We considered, first, the power of the particular group or person as it is rated relative to the ratings it receives at other institutions and, second, the power of the particular group or person as it ranks relative to the power of other groups or persons at the same university. We performed similar analyses for the goals. For the sake of simplicity, the findings of all the analyses are presented and discussed together.

In the case of two of the power-holders—the president and the vice-president—neither type of analysis produced any findings. The reason is simply that in both cases, the power is a constant: The president and vice-president always receive high ratings and fall in the top third of the power structure. It does not follow, of course, that all presidents and vice-presidents are equally powerful; our respondents were not asked to compare their chief officers with those of other institutions, but rather to rate them in comparison with other power groups at their own institutions.

Regents

Since regents almost always rank in the top third of the power structure, findings were sparse and, in the case of the within-university analysis, nonexistent. *Table 13* presents the few findings that resulted from the across-universities comparison. Where

TABLE 13

THE RELATIONSHIP BETWEEN THE POWER OF REGENTS AND PERCEIVED
UNIVERSITY GOALS

GOALS	POWER ACROSS UNIVERSITIES	
	1	2
OUTPUT GOALS:		
Student-Expressive		
1–Cultivate student's intellect	− .449	—
SUPPORT GOALS:		
Adaptation		
20–Educate to utmost high school graduates	.463	.543
23–Keep costs down	—	.495
Motivation		
36–Give faculty maximum opportunity to pursue careers	− .501	− .497
38–Protect students' right of inquiry	− .492	− .509
39–Protect students' right of action	− .453	—

1 = across-universities goals analysis   2 = within-university goals analysis

the regents have power, the goal of developing the student's intellect tends to be rated low (although it is not ranked low relative to other goals at the institution). Moreover, the two students' rights goals—of inquiry and of action—are not emphasized, nor is it considered important to give the faculty maximum opportunity to pursue their own careers. Indeed, the only goals that receive relatively great stress are those of educating all legally qualified high school graduates and of keeping costs down.

Legislators and the State Government

These two groups are considered together because the findings for both were highly similar. The explanation is obvious: One of the primary ways in which the state government makes itself felt in the academic community is through its legislators and their enactments. The results of the analysis for legislators are given in *Table 14*.

The same goals, with a few exceptions, appear in both types of analyses. That is, the goal structure is essentially the same when the legislators are rated as having a great influence relative to their influence at other universities and when they are ranked high relative to other power groups within the particular university.

The picture that emerges is a rather grim one, from the scholar's point of view. The three student-expressive intellective goals, and the related instrumental goal of training the students for scholarship, are subordinated, as are the more elevated of the direct service goals: disseminating new ideas and preserving the cultural heritage. On the other hand, practical output goals—preparing students for useful careers, carrying on applied research, and assisting citizens through extension services—are given priority.

With respect to support goals, nonselective admissions policies obtain, undergraduate instruction is emphasized at the cost of encouraging students to go on to graduate work, and precedence is given to providing student activities and involving students in university government, whereas the goal of protecting their right of inquiry is slighted.

The other emphasized goals are consistent with what one would expect from state legislators: concern about expenditures (keeping costs down) and about smooth functioning (keeping harmony among various parts of the university, making sure the

TABLE 14

THE RELATIONSHIP BETWEEN THE POWER OF STATE LEGISLATORS AND PERCEIVED
UNIVERSITY GOALS

GOAL	POWER ACROSS UNIVERSITIES		POWER WITHIN UNIVERSITY	
	1	2	1	2
OUTPUT GOALS:				
Student-Expressive				
1–Cultivate student's intellect..	−.704	−.769	−.693	−.782
3–Affect student with great ideas	−.674	−.721	−.604	−.665
4–Develop student's objectivity	−.628	−.750	−.618	−.708
Student-Instrumental				
6–Prepare students for useful careers.................	.566	.703	.469	.673
8–Train students for scholarship/research............	−.473	—	−.547	—
Research				
12–Carry on applied research...	—	.596	—	.540
Direct Service				
14-Assist citizens through extension programs............	.692	.673	.648	.625
16–Disseminate new ideas......	−.482	−.495	−.527	−.514
17–Preserve cultural heritage....	−.496	−.575	—	—
SUPPORT GOALS:				
Adaptation				
19–Ensure favor of validating bodies.................	—	.739	—	.767
20–Educate to utmost high school graduates.........	.804	.819	.767	.766
21–Accept good students only...	−.782	−.900	−.840	−.924
22–Satisfy area needs..........	.602	.480	.630	.558
23–Keep costs down...........	.546	.542	.562	.623
Management				
27–Involve students in university government..............	.567	—	.582	—
29–Keep harmony.............	.531	—	.480	—
31–Emphasize undergraduate instruction....	.605	—	.585	—
32–Encourage graduate work....	−.540	—	−.622	—
33–Ensure efficient goal attainment...................	—	.561	—	—
Motivation				
35–Protect academic freedom...	−.654	—	−.620	—
36–Give faculty maximum opportunity to pursue careers...	−.588	−.525	−.624	−.597
37–Provide student activities...	.501	.628	.451	.614
38–Protect students' right of inquiry.................	−.560	−.512	−.547	—
Position				
42–Maintain top quality in all programs...............	—	—	−.512	—
43–Maintain top quality in important programs.........	—	—	−.478	—
45–Keep up to date...........	—	—	−.469	—
46–Increase or maintain prestige	−.656	—	−.649	—
47–Preserve institutional character.....................	−.482	—	−.487	—

1 = across-universities goals analysis   2 = within-university goals analysis

university is run by those who can most efficiently attain its goals).

The faculty suffers somewhat at universities where legislators have considerable power: Protecting academic freedom and giving the faculty maximum opportunity to pursue their careers receive relatively little emphasis.

The findings for the position goals (particularly in the within-university analysis) suggest that at such universities, little attention is given to those matters which concern the more prestigious institutions: maintaining top quality in all programs or in those programs considered particularly important, keeping up to date, increasing or maintaining prestige, and preserving the character of the institution.

In situations where the state government has power, the perceived goal structure is essentially the same, except that the student-expressive goal of developing character and the direct service goal of serving as a cultural center for the community are added to the list of casualties.

Private Agencies

No particular goal structure emerges at universities where the power of private agencies is rated high relative to other universities. The few scattered findings shown in *Table 15* indicate that cultivating the student's intellect and ensuring the confidence of contributors are emphasized, whereas assisting citizens through extension programs and accepting all legally qualified high school graduates are not. However, when we consider the situation in which private agencies have considerable influence relative to other groups within the university, we find a definite goal structure.

Of the output goals, those relating to the student's intellectual and scholarly development are emphasized, pure research is elevated over applied research, and the more practical service goals lose out to the goal of preserving the cultural heritage.

The pattern is similar with respect to the support goals: There is a clear tendency to emphasize what we have called elitist goals, those connected with the more prestigious and graduate-oriented universities (except that position goals are not so strongly emphasized) at the cost of the "service" goals. The most noteworthy findings are the very high negative *gamma* ($-.900$) associated with the goal of educating all qualified high school graduates and,

TABLE 15
THE RELATIONSHIP BETWEEN THE POWER OF PRIVATE AGENCIES AND PERCEIVED
UNIVERSITY GOALS

GOAL	POWER ACROSS UNIVERSITIES		POWER WITHIN UNIVERSITY	
	1	2	1	2
OUTPUT GOALS:				
Student-Expressive				
1–Cultivate students' intellect..	—	.493	.767	.898
3–Affect student with great ideas..................	—	—	.816	—
4–Develop student's objectivity	—	—	.649	.841
Student-Instrumental				
6–Prepare students for useful careers.................	—	—	−.654	−.625
8–Train students for scholarship/research............	—	—	.641	.743
Research				
11–Carry on pure research......	—	—	.519	—
12–Carry on applied research...	—	—	−.543	−.653
Direct Service				
14–Assist citizens through extension programs............	−.470	−.473	−.783	−.695
15–Provide community cultural leadership..............	—	—	—	−.519
17–Preserve cultural heritage....	—	—	—	.640
SUPPORT GOALS:				
Adaptation				
18–Ensure confidence of contributors.................	.629	—	.543	—
19–Ensure favor of validating bodies................	—	—	−.549	−.598
20–Educate to utmost high school graduates................	−.634	−.567	−.900	−.779
21–Accept good students only...	—	—	.745	.813
22–Satisfy area needs..........	—	—	−.695	—
23–Keep costs down..........	—	—	−.571	—
Management				
27–Involve students in university government..........	—	—	−.748	—
29–Keep harmony.............	—	—	−.703	—
31–Emphasize undergraduate instruction..............	—	—	−.603	—
32–Encourage graduate work....	—	—	.692	.666
Motivation				
35–Protect academic freedom...	—	—	.539	—
36–Give faculty maximum opportunity to pursue careers...	—	—	.509	.603
37–Provide student activities....	—	—	−.594	−.652
38–Protect students' right of inquiry.................	—	—	.531	—
Position				
46–Increase or maintain prestige.	—	—	.509	—

1 = across-universities goals analysis   2 = within-university goals analysis

again, the emphasis on ensuring the confidence (and hence support) of contributors. That there is considerable concern with this latter goal at universities which depend on the support of private agencies is not at all surprising.

Federal Government

Table 16 presents the findings for the across-universities analysis of the relationship between the power of the Federal government and perceived university goals. The within-university analysis yielded almost no findings—an indication that the Federal government's having considerable influence relative to other power-holders at the same institution has little effect on the institution's goals.

At universities where the power of the Federal government is rated high relative to the ratings it receives at other institutions, the three student-expressive intellective goals tend to receive little attention, carrying on applied research and ensuring the confidence of contributors are emphasized, involving students in university government is considered important, but protecting and

TABLE 16

THE RELATIONSHIP BETWEEN THE POWER OF THE FEDERAL GOVERNMENT AND PERCEIVED UNIVERSITY GOALS

GOALS	POWER ACROSS UNIVERSITIES	
	1	2
OUTPUT GOALS:		
Student-Expressive		
1–Cultivate student's intellect	−.552	−.607
3–Affect student with great ideas	−.492	−.607
4–Develop student's objectivity	—	−.544
Research		
12–Carry on applied research	—	.504
SUPPORT GOALS:		
Adaptation		
18–Ensure confidence of contributors	—	.787
Management		
27–Involve students in university government	.470	—
Motivation		
38–Protect students' right of inquiry	—	−.475
39–Protect students' right of action	−.461	—

1 = across-universities goals analysis   2 = within-university goals analysis

facilitating their right of inquiry and their right to advocate and carry out political and social action are not.

The very paucity of the findings is meaningful. Our analysis, which seems to support Orlans's conclusion that Federal grants do not have much effect on the structure of emphases at universities,[3] should serve to reassure those who see the Federal government as some kind of ogre, distorting and perverting the American system of higher education.

Deans of Graduate Schools

With this group, too, findings were sparse, though just why this should be so is puzzling, particularly since the analyses for deans of liberal arts and of professional schools were fruitful. At universities where the dean of the graduate school is rated as having

[3] Harold Orlans, *Effects of Federal Programs on Higher Education* (Washington: The Brookings Institution, 1962).

TABLE 17

THE RELATIONSHIP BETWEEN THE POWER OF DEANS OF LIBERAL ARTS AND PERCEIVED UNIVERSITY GOALS

GOAL	POWER ACROSS UNIVERSITIES		POWER WITHIN UNIVERSITY	
	1	2	1	2
OUTPUT GOALS:				
Student -Expressive				
1–Cultivate student's intellect..	.695	.644	.758	.590
3–Affect student with great ideas..................	.605	—	.716	.723
4–Develop student's objectivity	.648	.750	.616	.773
Student-Instrumental				
6–Prepare students for useful careers.................	—	−.821	—	−.650
8–Train students for scholarship/research............	.621	—	—	—
Research				
11–Carry on pure research......	.554	.511	—	—
12–Carry on applied research...	−.498	−.692	—	—
Direct Service				
13–Provide special adult training	−.459	−.532	—	—
14–Assist citizens through extension programs...........	−.532	−.692	−.533	−.622
16–Disseminate new ideas......	.500	—	.518	—
17–Preserve cultural heritage....	.565	.498	.613	.549
SUPPORT GOALS:				
Adaptation				
19–Ensure favor of validating bodies.................	—	−.738	—	−.642
20–Educate to utmost high school graduates...............	−.489	−.476	—	−.514

considerable say in the big decisions, doing pure research and preserving the character of the institution are emphasized, but keeping costs down is not. Perhaps graduate school deans simply accept the fact that what they are doing will cost money and so refuse to worry about it too much.

Deans of Liberal Arts

In contrast to graduate school deans, deans of liberal arts seem to have considerable influence on goal structure. Their values are what one would expect from the very title of the position. As *Table 17* indicates, the goals associated with a powerful dean of liberal arts (considered across institutions) are the scholarly and elitist goals as opposed to practical and somewhat anti-intellectual goals. The student's intellect, objectivity, knowledgability about great ideas, and scholarly skills are cultivated, pure research is exalted over applied research, and the university is

TABLE 17 *continued*

GOALS	POWER ACROSS UNIVERSITIES		POWER WITHIN UNIVERSITY	
	1	2	1	2
SUPPORT GOALS: *continued*				
21–Accept good students only...	.524	.615	.550	−.554
22–Satisfy area needs..........	−.487	−.610	—	−.570
23–Keep costs down..........	−.521	−.616	—	—
Management				
25–Reward for contribution to profession...............	.624	.530	—	—
31–Emphasize undergraduate instruction................	−.473	−1.000	—	—
32–Encourage graduate work....	.618	—	—	—
33–Ensure efficient goal attainment....................	.565	—	—	—
Motivation				
35–Protect academic freedom...	.593	—	.547	1.000
36–Give faculty maximum opportunity to pursue careers...	.634	.559	—	—
37–Provide student activities....	—	−.654	−.526	−.593
38–Protect students' right of inquiry.................	.722	.710	.640	.646
39–Protect students' right of action.................	—	—	.516	—
Position				
42–Maintain top quality in all programs...............	.641	.618	.530	—
43–Maintain top quality in important programs.........	.590	—	.547	—
45–Keep up to date..........	.563	—	—	—
46–Increase or maintain prestige	.505	—	—	—

1 = across-universities goals analysis   2 = within-university goals analysis

viewed as a center for disseminating new ideas and preserving the cultural heritage rather than an agency for providing special adult training and extension services.

These elitist tendencies are reflected too in some of the support goals connected with students. Admissions policies are selective, graduate work is encouraged at the expense of emphasis on undergraduate instruction (which invariably ranks in the bottom third of goals), the academic and political rights of students are considered important, but the provision of a full program of activities is not.

Similarly, the faculty's interests and well-being are given priority. Position goals having to do with the quality of the academic program and with prestige receive high ratings (though they are not emphasized out of proportion to other goals within the university).

On the other hand, such workaday goals as ensuring the favorable appraisal of validating bodies, satisfying area needs, and keeping costs down are given little attention. Interestingly, the goal of making sure that the university is run by those selected for their ability to attain its goals in the most efficient manner possible *is* emphasized; it will be recalled that persons at the more productive, prestigious, graduate-oriented universities put a low value on this goal.

When we consider situations where the dean of liberal arts has considerable say in decison making relative to other groups within the institution, the findings are fewer. The two research goals and all four management goals, for instance, drop out. However, the over-all impression that one gets of the dean of liberal arts as a champion of scholarly values is still present.

Deans of Professional Schools

Although the picture of the dean of liberal arts that emerges from the analyses contains few surprises, it is somewhat startling to discover that the goals associated with powerful deans of professional schools are much the same, at least in the across-institutions analysis (*Table 18*). The number of significant goals is smaller: For instance, affecting the student permanently with great ideas and protecting his right of political action are not necessarily emphasized at universities where deans of professional schools have considerable influence, nor are the position goals of keeping up to date and maintaining prestige. By and large, however, the same goals are significant in both analyses, and always in the same direction.

In some instances, the goals seem odd and even inappropriate. For example, preparing students for useful careers, carrying on applied research, assisting citizens through extension programs, ensuring the favorable appraisal of validating bodies, and satisfying area needs—all matters that one would expect to be of con-

TABLE 18

The Relationship Between the Power of Deans of Professional Schools and Perceived University Goals

Goals	Power Across Universities	
	1	2
OUTPUT GOALS:		
Student-Expressive		
1–Cultivate student's intellect	.523	.578
4–Develop student's objectivity	.528	.611
Student-Instrumental		
6–Prepare students for useful careers	—	−.637
8–Train students for scholarship/research	.516	—
Research		
12–Carry on applied research	—	−.493
Direct Service		
14–Assist citizens through extension programs	—	−.479
15–Provide community cultural leadership	—	−.508
SUPPORT GOALS:		
Adaptation		
19–Ensure favor of validating bodies	—	−.590
20–Educate to utmost high school graduates	−.440	−.551
21–Accept good students only	.579	.595
22–Satisfy area needs	—	−.501
23–Keep costs down	−.443	−.596
Management		
25–Reward for contribution to profession	.583	—
32–Encourage graduate work	.572	—
33–Ensure efficient goal attainment	.571	—
Motivation		
35–Protect academic freedom	.509	—
36–Give faculty maximum opportunity to pursue careers	.566	.480
37–Provide student activities	—	−.598
38–Protect students' right of inquiry	.552	.589
Position		
42–Maintain top quality in all programs	.570	.580
43–Maintain top quality in important programs	.489	—

1 = across-universities goals analysis   2 = within-university goals analysis

cern to deans of professional schools—tend to be given low priority. The goal of emphasizing undergraduate instruction invariably ranks in the bottom third.

TABLE 19

THE RELATIONSHIP BETWEEN THE POWER OF CHAIRMEN AND PERCEIVED UNIVERSITY GOALS

GOALS	POWER ACROSS UNIVERSITIES	
	1	2
OUTPUT GOALS:		
Student-Expressive		
1–Cultivate student's intellect	.603	—
4–Develop student's objectivity	.585	.596
Student-Instrumental		
6–Prepare students for useful careers	—	−.741
8–Train students for scholarship/research	—	.818
Research		
11–Carry on pure research	.568	.622
12–Carry on applied research	—	−.483
Direct Service		
14–Assist citizens through extension programs	—	−.518
16–Disseminate new ideas	.661	.477
17–Preserve cultural heritage	.478	—
SUPPORT GOALS:		
Adaptation		
19–Ensure favor of validating bodies	—	−.759
21–Accept good students only	.497	.509
22–Satisfy area needs	−.488	−.660
23–Keep costs down	−.510	−.668
Management		
25–Reward for contribution to profession	.811	.663
26–Involve faculty in university government	.507	—
28–Run university democratically	.595	.545
32–Encourage graduate work	.537	—
33–Ensure efficient goal attainment	.672	—
34–Let will of faculty prevail	.750	.699
Motivation		
35–Protect academic freedom	.664	—
36–Give faculty maximum opportunity to pursue careers	.753	.621
37–Provide student activities	—	−.574
38–Protect students' right of inquiry	.714	.683
39–Protect students' right of action	.524	—
Position		
42–Maintain top quality in all programs	.768	.683
43–Maintain top quality in important programs	.577	—
44–Maintain balanced quality in all programs	.528	—
45–Keep up to date	.606	—

1 = across-universities goals analysis   2 = within-university goals analysis

Judging from these results, the fears of those who regard the dean of a professional school as narrow and restrictive in his outlook, overly concerned with his own particular field, and hostile to the liberal arts, seem to be unfounded. This conclusion must be tempered somewhat, however, in light of our failure to turn up any results in the within-university analysis. Apparently, no particular goal structure is associated with universities where deans of professional schools have considerable power relative to other persons or groups at the institution, but only with universities where they are powerful compared with deans of professional schools at other universities.

Departmental Chairmen

Because the power of departmental chairmen is virtually a constant (they ranked in the middle third of the distribution at 65 of the 68 universities), no significant findings emerged from the within-university analysis (see *Table 19*). When we compare ratings across universities, however, we find that at institutions where chairmen as a group are perceived as having considerable say in decision making, the goal structure resembles that of universities where deans of liberal arts or of professional schools are powerful. The same scholarly and elitist goals are emphasized, and the more practical considerations unemphasized.

Where chairmen are powerful (relative to their counterparts at other universities), the well-being of the faculty receives heavy stress: Academic freedom and the professional development of the faculty are matters of concern. The management goals of involving the faculty in university government, making sure that the university is run democratically, and seeing to it that the will of the faculty prevails on all important issues receive emphasis here (as they did not in the case of deans). Moreover, the students' right to advocate and participate in political and social action is stressed, along with their right of inquiry.

The findings for chairmen resemble even more closely the findings for faculty—not surprising, since chairmen usually regard themselves, and are regarded, as faculty members.

Faculty

The power of the faculty is a subject of obvious interest. Many professors feel that they have very little power and are inclined to lament this fact (if fact it is). On the other hand, our interviews indicate, and the literature emphasizes, that faculty members have little interest in administering the university or even in formulating policy; in any event, they are disinclined to take the time to do so. Administrators often speak of the "working faculty," those faculty members who are willing to serve on committees and to assist in policy-making activities. It is worth asking, then, how a powerful faculty affects the goal structure of a university. What are those universities like where the faculty is perceived as having a great deal of say in decision making? Is there anything distinctive about them?

Table 20 presents the results of the analyses. It has already been pointed out that the findings for faculty resemble the findings for chairmen, and that these in turn are very similar to the findings for deans of liberal arts and of professional schools. On

TABLE 20

THE RELATIONSHIP BETWEEN THE POWER OF THE FACULTY AND PERCEIVED UNIVERSITY GOALS

GOALS	POWER ACROSS UNIVERSITIES		POWER WITHIN UNIVERSITY	
	1	2	1	2
OUTPUT GOALS:				
Student-Expressive				
1–Cultivate student's intellect..	.476	—	—	—
2–Produce well-rounded student	—	−.637	—	—
4–Develop student's objectivity	.564	—	.666	—
Student-Instrumental				
6–Prepare students for useful careers..................	−.544	−.703	—	—
7–Prepare students for status/ leadership..............	—	−.524	—	—
8–Train students for scholarship/research............	.528	—	—	1.000
9–Cultivate student's taste....	−.495	—	—	—
10–Prepare student for citizenship....................	—	−.644	—	−.790
Research				
11–Carry on pure research......	.589	.595	—	—
12–Carry on applied research....	—	−.598	—	—
Direct Service				
13–Provide special adult training	—	−.601	—	—
14–Assist citizens through extension programs............	—	−.526	—	—
16–Disseminate new ideas......	.537	.503	—	—
17–Preserve cultural heritage...	.452	—	—	—
SUPPORT GOALS:				
Adaptation				
19–Ensure favor of validating bodies..................	—	−.844	—	−.791
21–Accept good students only...	.474	.501	—	—

the whole, then, it would seem that the faculty suffers little at universities where deans rather than faculty have the power; the goals pursued are essentially the same. They tend to be the elitist, scholarly, profession-oriented goals rather than practical, community service goals. Not surprisingly, goals that specifically touch on the direct interests of the faculty prevail. Involving the faculty in university government, running the university democratically, and giving the faculty final say in important decisions all relate to the role of the faculty in policy making. Rewarding faculty on the basis of their contribution to their profession (rather than to the institution) and giving them maximum opportunity to pursue their careers as they see fit relate to their professional ambitions. The protection of academic freedom

TABLE 20 *continued*

GOALS	POWER ACROSS UNIVERSITIES		POWER WITHIN UNIVERSITY	
	1	2	1	2
SUPPORT GOALS: *continued*				
22–Satisfy area needs	—	−.574	—	−.727
23–Keep costs down	−.526	−.639	—	—
Management				
25–Reward for contribution to profession	.680	—	—	—
26–Involve faculty in university government	.878	.833	.935	.917
28–Run university democratically	.821	.836	.834	.912
29–Keep harmony	—	−1.000	—	—
31–Emphasize undergraduate instruction	—	−1.000	—	−.952
33–Ensure efficient goal attainment	.506	—	—	—
34–Let will of faculty prevail	.946	.965	1.000	.938
Motivation				
35–Protect academic freedom	.803	1.000	.764	—
36–Give faculty maximum opportunity to pursue careers	.775	.735	.868	.793
37–Provide student activities	—	−.566	—	—
38–Protect students' right of inquiry	.766	.718	.868	.682
39–Protect students' right of action	.656	.830	.868	.819
41–Develop pride in university	—	—	—	−.701
Position				
42–Maintain top quality in all programs	.594	—	—	—
43–Maintain top quality in important programs	.456	—	—	—
45–Keep up to date	.446	—	.709	—

1 = across-universities goals analysis   2 = within-university goals analysis

(which, in the across-institutions analysis of power structure, always ranks in the top third of the goal structure) has an obvious bearing on their interests.

One striking difference between this analysis and previous analyses is that certain negatively related goals appear here. That is, at universities where the faculty has considerable power (relative to their power at other universities), low priority is very definitely assigned to such goals as producing a well-rounded student, providing him with the skills and experiences that will facilitate upward mobility, cultivating his taste, and preparing him for citizenship. Similarly, certain support goals are subordinated. Keeping harmony and emphasizing undergraduate instruction are invariably ranked in the bottom third of goals.

The findings for the within-university analysis are much sparser, primarily because the power of the faculty comes close to being a constant. Of the 68 universities in the sample, the faculty was rated in the bottom third of the power structure at two, in the middle third at 57, and in the top third at nine. The relationships, therefore, were determined by the small group of eleven universities which fell outside the middle group, and consequently we cannot place too much credence in them. Nonetheless, there is a consistent relationship between the power of the faculty and the emphasis placed on training students for scholarship and research. Making sure that the will of the faculty prevails in all important decisions is also given heavy weight. One goal not significant in the across-institutions analysis crops up here: that of developing pride in the university, which—consistent with the professional as opposed to institutional orientation of the faculty —is given low priority.

In short, essentially the same goal emphases are associated with powerful deans, powerful chairmen, and a powerful faculty, though the tendency to stress certain goals relating to faculty authority and well-being is more marked where faculty is powerful, as is the tendency to regard certain goals as unimportant.

Students, Parents, Citizens, and Alumni

When we examine the goal structures associated with the power of students, parents, citizens, and alumni, we draw almost a complete blank, primarily because these groups are generally perceived as having little power. They have impact only on scattered goals. For example, such slight differences as are found in the power of students are related to the goals of letting the will of the faculty prevail and involving students in university government. Both these findings may be attributable to chance, though the latter makes good common sense. The power of the much-feared alumni is related to the goals of preparing the student to occupy a high-status position, ensuring the favorable appraisal of validating bodies, providing student activities, and producing a well-rounded student.

In brief, those who feel that these groups are evil geniuses operating behind the scenes to the detriment of the university have little cause for alarm.

SUMMARY

American universities are remarkably similar in their power structures. At almost all institutions, the president, vice-president, and regents are perceived as having a great deal of say in making big decisions, whereas alumni, students, citizens, and parents are perceived as having little or no say. Such differences as exist in power structure are attributable chiefly to type of control, although a university's emphasis on graduate work, its quality, and its location also influence its goal structure to some extent.

Nonetheless, the differences in power structure that were revealed are important ones, insofar as the goals that the university pursues are concerned. In our analyses, there seems to be a clear split between those institutions where legislators, the state government, and (to a much lesser degree) the regents have power and those where deans of liberal arts or of professional schools, departmental chairmen, faculty, and private agencies have power. The distinction is between those goals that reflect "service" values, on the one hand, and elitist values, on the other. Although there are, to be sure, certain idiosyncratic findings connected with each group, we can safely generalize that at universities where deans, chairmen, faculty, or private agencies have considerable influence on decision making, scholarly values and faculty interests are given precedence, somewhat to the detriment of undergraduate instruction, of day-to-day practical considerations, and of the practical service mission of the university.

Chapter 5

ADMINISTRATORS AND FACULTY: CONFLICT OVER GOALS?

As was pointed out in the first chapter, the growth in the size and complexity of collegiate institutions during recent years has presumably led to an increase in the numbers and power of the adminstrative staff. This development is viewed with alarm by many people, who feel that administrators may force their own values and concerns on the faculty and undermine the true purposes of the institution. Two questions are involved here. Do administrators actually have more power than faculty members do? If so, do they misuse that power by pursuing goals which the faculty regards as trivial or objectionable and by neglecting goals which the faculty regards as appropriate and desirable?

The analysis of the power structure of the American university would suggest that the answer to the first question is: Yes, administrators do have more power than faculty members, and the higher the rank of the administrator, the greater his power. The single exception is that the faculty is usually rated as having more power than do departmental chairmen as a group. Otherwise, the hierarchy of real power parallels the formal academic hierarchy, from the president at the top through the vice-president and the deans and down to chairmen and faculty members.

An examination of the relationships between power structure and perceived goals suggests at least a tentative answer to the second question. The remarkable similarity in the goal emphases of universities where deans are powerful and those where the faculty is powerful implies that the dominance of administrators, though a reality, is not a threat. But more direct evidence is needed before this assertion can be made with confidence. In this chapter, then, attention is devoted to comparing faculty and administrators, with reference to their similarities and differences in (1) backgrounds and personal characteristics, (2) perceptions of what goals are being emphasized at their institutions, and (3) views of what goals *should* be emphasized.

BACKGROUND AND PERSONAL CHARACTERISTICS

Of the total sample of 7,224 who returned usable questionnaires, 4,494 (roughly 62 percent) were administrators, and 2,730 (roughly 38 percent) were faculty members. In addition to indicating their goal perceptions and preferences, respondents furnished information about themselves—e.g., age, marital and family status, church affiliation, educational attainment (see Section 9 of the questionnaire, *Appendix C,* page 155)—which was used in making these comparisons.

It should come as no surprise to learn that administrators tend to be older than faculty members. Several of the other characteristics that distinguish them from faculty are related to their being older: They have a higher total income, a greater proportion of which comes from consulting and writing; they are more likely to be divorced, separated, or widowed; and they have more education. This last finding is probably attributable not only to their greater age, but also to our having classified departmental chairmen as administrators; chairmen as a group tend to have attained high academic degrees.

Other background characteristics that distinguish administrators from faculty members are not related to age but seem rather to suggest that administrators as a group more nearly approach what may be called the traditional American norm, whereas faculty members tend to be more heterogeneous and diverse in their backgrounds. For instance, administrators are more likely to be Lutheran, Congregationalist, or Episcopalian than Catholic or Jewish. On the other hand, the faculty as a group tends to have a higher proportion of women and non-whites. Faculty members are also more likely than are administrators to have foreign-born fathers, to have been born outside the United States themselves, to have been born in urban areas, and to have lived abroad or in an urban area when they were young. Finally, they received their degrees more recently, a trait obviously attributable to their relative youth.

THE PERCEIVED GOALS OF FACULTY
AND OF ADMINISTRATORS

It is conceivable that these differences in background and personal characteristics, though slight, may result in differences in perceptions: That is, the two groups may diverge in how they see and interpret a situation. But a comparison of their responses to the question of what goals their universities are actually pursuing suggests that few such discrepancies exist. They agree in their views of the relative emphasis placed on 34 of the 47 goals, but administrators give higher ratings to the following 13 perceived goals:

1. Produce a student who has had his intellect cultivated to the maximum.
2. Assist students to develop objectivity about themselves and their beliefs and hence examine those beliefs critically.
3. Develop the character of students so that they can make sound, correct moral choices.
4. Produce a student who is able to perform his citizenship responsibilities effectively.
5. Retain staff in the face of inducements from other institutions.
6. Make sure that the university is run democratically insofar as that is feasible.
7. Base rewards on the contribution that the person makes to the institution.
8. Make sure that on *all* important issues, the will of the faculty prevails.
9. Protect the faculty's right to academic freedom.
10. Protect the students' right of inquiry.
11. Protect the students' right to advocate or take direct political or social action.
12. Develop faculty loyalty to the university.
13. Maintain top quality in those programs felt to be especially important.

The views of faculty and administrators about the relative emphasis given to these 13 goals differed very little. The *gamma* was less than .176, a figure which in our other analyses was regarded as too low to be significant. The differences that do exist seem attributable to the different vantage points of the two groups. The higher ratings which administrators give to the four output goals relating to students may reflect more optimism than accuracy, considering their lack of contact with students in the classroom. The faculty member, more exposed to the blandishment of other universities, would naturally be more inclined to feel that his own institution is not offering all the inducements that it might to hold him.

More than half of the disagreements between the two groups concern goals related to management and motivation and thus center around how the university is run and what it does to keep students and faculty happy. Given the different functions of the two groups, it is not surprising that their perceptions of the emphasis placed on such goals should differ, though it is impossible to say whose view is the more accurate. One might offhand suppose that since administrators are more deeply involved in the governance of the institution, their perceptions of the priority accorded to such goals as running the university democratically and seeing to it that the will of the faculty prevails on all important issues are more likely to be valid. But one could argue with equal force that their very involvement may distort their view. The same arguments apply to the faculty's perceptions of the motivation goals of protecting the faculty's academic freedom and the students' rights of inquiry and of action and of developing faculty loyalty to the institution. Disagreement over the position goal of maintaining top quality in the most important programs may result from the administrator's wider perspective of the total academic program.

The responses of administrators of different ranks—chairmen, deans, vice-presidents, and presidents—were compared to see whether perceptions change as rank rises. The results were essentially the same as those in the previous comparison, except that there were no differences among ranks on the perceived goals of developing the student's character or developing the faculty's loyalty to the institution. The higher ranking administrators tend to give higher ratings than did lower ranking administrators to all the other goals in the preceding list plus two others: disseminating new ideas and involving the faculty in university government. But the degree of disagreement was very small; the *gammas* did not exceed .138.

THE PREFERRED GOALS OF FACULTY AND OF ADMINISTRATORS

The goal preferences of the two groups are particularly crucial in answering the second of the questions raised at the beginning of this chapter. If the preferred goal systems of the two groups contrast sharply, and if administrators are in a position to impose their preferences on the faculty, then the viewers-with-alarm may have some justification for their anxieties about the power of administrators. If, on the other hand, the two groups essentially agree on what the goals of the university should be, such fears are less warranted. Moreover, goal preferences are intimately related to values, and disagreements over goals probably reflect deeper conflicts that may result in disharmony and disruption within an organization.

But again, agreement was high, and where disagreement did exist, it was slight. Administrators tended to place a slightly higher value on only the following goals:

1. Develop the character of students so that they can make sound, correct moral choices.
2. Make a good consumer of the student.
3. Produce a student who is able to perform his citizenship responsibilities effectively.
4. Serve as a center for the preservation of the cultural heritage.
5. Ensure the confidence and support of those who contribute substantially to the university.
6. Satisfy the special needs of the immediate geographical region.
7. Retain staff in the face of inducements from other institutions.
8. Base rewards on the contribution that the person makes to the institution.
9. Make sure that the university is run by those best able to attain its goals in the most efficient manner possible.
10. Develop faculty loyalty to the university.
11. Develop pride in the university.
12. Maintain top quality in the programs felt to be especially important.
13. Increase or maintain the prestige of the university.

The faculty tends to place a higher value on only the following goals:

14. Make sure that on *all* important issues (not only curriculum), the will of the faculty prevails.
15. Make the university a place in which faculty have maximum opportunity to pursue their careers in a manner satisfactory to them by their own criteria.

Administrators tend to value more highly than do faculty members the goals relating to the student's moral development and his roles of consumer and citizen. This difference probably results from the more purely scholarly orientation of the faculty, which tends to scorn all student output goals except those connected with intellectual development and scholarly skills. The support goals on the list reflect the administrator's greater concern with the well-being and reputation of the institution and with the need for satisfying certain outside constituencies such as the citizens of the local area and potential contributors.

The two goals that faculty assign a higher value are directly related to their own interests. Their feeling that the faculty should have the final way say on all important matters of university government is balanced against the administrators' feeling that the university should be run by those who can attain its goals most efficiently, while the professionalism (and personal ambition) reflected in the priority that faculty members would give to allowing faculty maximum opportunity to pursue their own careers contrasts with the local and institutional orientation of administrators.

Where there is disagreement over the value of a particular goal, there also tends to be disagreement over the emphasis it receives. Common to both lists are seven goals: developing the student's character, preparing him for citizenship, holding staff, rewarding faculty for their contribution to the institution, developing faculty loyalty to the institution, maintaining top quality in important programs, and letting the will of the faculty prevail. With respect to the first six, it is possible that because administrators value these goals highly and (in their own view) expend considerable effort pursuing them, they may believe that they are actually receiving more emphasis; this expenditure of effort may not, however, be visible to the faculty. A converse explanation can be given for the appearance of the last goal: because of the high value they accord it, whatever emphasis is given will fall short of the ideal, as conceived by the faculty.

As a check on these findings, the goal preferences of administrators of different ranks were compared. Again, results were similar, except that there were no differences among different ranks in the value assigned to developing the student's taste and ensuring efficient goal attainment. The tendency to give high ratings to the other goals on the list for administrators becomes more pronounced at each step in the hierarchy. Moreover, the higher the rank of the administrator, the higher is his regard for the goals of seeing to it that the student is affected permanently by great ideas, keeping costs down, and providing student activities. Lower ranking administrators resemble faculty in their preferences for the goals of letting the will of the faculty prevail and of allowing faculty members maximum opportunity to pursue their careers.

But it should be stressed again that the few differences that exist in the values and attitudes of administrators and faculty, as revealed in their ratings of preferred goals, are too slight to warrant any inference of deep-seated conflict. All three comparisons—of background and personal characteristics, of perceived goals, and of preferred goals—suggests that administrators and faculty are not such different breeds as they are sometimes assumed to be. They value and work toward essentially the same goals. In short, the power of administrators does not seem to jeopardize the interests of the faculty.

CHAPTER 6

SUMMARY

Although it is generally agreed that the modern university is among the most important institutions in our society, no such consensus exists on its role and purposes. Despite the many attempts to define what this complex organization is and to prescribe how it should behave, there has been little systematic or empirical study of how the university is administered and how it functions. The present study represents one such attempt.

Every segment of society may have its own answers to these questions, but obviously some people's views are more important than others, because they have a direct effect on the direction the university takes. Assuming (perhaps oversimply, given the diffuseness of the university as an organization) that power and influence accompany office, then the most important group to study, if one is to arrive at an improved understanding, is the administrators who have the primary responsibility for making and effecting decisions.

This study focuses on university administrators and on their perceptions of what the goals of the university are, what the goals should be, and what persons or groups are in positions of real power. In addition, it examines the views of faculty members on these questions, in order to test the validity of the common assertion that faculty and administrators have different points of view and different values and that therefore the decision-making power of a centralized administration is an inimical influence on the university. A second purpose was to learn how the global characteristics and the power structure of the university are related to its goal emphases and to the goal values of its leading personnel. Finally, faculty and administrators were compared to learn how they differ in background and personal characteristics and in their views of what the goals of the university are and should be.

DESIGN OF THE STUDY

Our basic research instrument was a mailed questionnaire which included a list of 47 goals. Among the unique features of this study

107

was, first, the length of the list (all too often studies of organizational goals have limited values because the listed goals are too general) and, second, the inclusion in the list of certain maintenance activities usually regarded as means rather than ends; these support goals are just as important and consume just as much attention and energy as the more widely accepted output goals of teaching, research, and service. Each respondent was asked to indicate, on a five-point scale, just how much emphasis he felt a given goal *received* at his institution and how much emphasis he felt it *should* receive. Thus, we were able to derive a *perceived* and a *preferred* goal structure both for the over-all sample and for each institution in the sample.

In another part of the questionnaire, the respondent was asked how much influence each of 16 agencies, groups, or persons had in making the big decisions at the university. This information was used to define the power structure—over-all and at each university in the sample. Background information about the respondents was also collected.[1]

Sixty-eight universities—both public and nondenominational private—constituted the basic sample for this study. Questionnaires were sent to presidents, vice-presidents, academic deans, nonacademic deans, department heads, and persons classified as directors; to members of governing boards; and to a 10 percent sample of faculty members at each institution. Of the approximately 16,000 questionnaires mailed out in 1964, about 7,200 usable returns (46 percent) were received, a gratifyingly high response rate considering the length of the questionnaire and the demanding jobs of the respondents.

UNIVERSITY GOAL STRUCTURES: THE ACTUAL AND THE IDEAL

Looking at the responses of the total sample, faculty and administrators alike, we find that the goal of protecting the faculty's academic freedom is at the head of the list; not only is it perceived as being the goal that receives the strongest emphasis (mean score: 3.90, on a scale of 1 to 5), but also it is regarded as the goal to be most highly valued (mean score: 4.33). Much as academic persons squabble among themselves

---

[1] The questionnaire contained several other sections—about the respondent's opinions on the workings of formal and informal organizations of the university, about his own career pattern, and about his feelings toward his job. These findings are not reported here, but will appear subsequently in professional journals.

about the meaning of "academic freedom," there is little question that those in higher education present a united front to the nonacademic world in defending its importance.

According to our respondents, goals related to students receive relatively little emphasis at American universities today, the one exception being that of training students for scholarship, research, and creative endeavor. But there is some feeling, apparently, that universities should pay more attention to educating the student: The goals of cultivating the student's intellect and developing his objectivity rank high on the list of preferred goals. Also upgraded are the goals of developing the student's character and citizenship abilities, affecting him with great ideas, and producing a well-rounded student. Our respondents feel, too, that more attention should be paid to protecting the students' right of inquiry, but not their right to advocate and take direct action— a goal which ranks low on both lists. But it is felt that too much attention is paid to preparing students for useful careers, facilitating their upward mobility, and providing a full round of student activities. The goals of involving students in university government and of cultivating taste are neither emphasized nor valued: They fall at the very bottom rank on both lists.

Emphasizing undergraduate instruction occupies the forty-fourth position on both lists, an indication that the low priority already accorded to this goal is felt to be appropriate. But, oddly enough, respondents feel that encouraging students to go into graduate work ought not to receive as much stress as it does.

Another upward shift from the perceived to the preferred list occurs in the case of three goals relating to having a local as opposed to a cosmopolitan orientation: basing rewards on the faculty member's contribution to the institution, developing the faculty's loyalty to the institution, and developing pride in the institution. The tendency to feel that these three goals should receive more emphasis than they do may reflect, in part, the problems that administrators have with faculty mobility, particularly, of course, with discouraging competent professors from leaving the university. It may also reflect dissatisfaction over the faculty's unwillingness to work for the good of the institution (rather than for their own profession and their advancement in it) by participating more fully in institutional affairs.

Both research goals drop sharply in ranking (although not in their mean scores, which, in the case of pure research, was rated higher as a preferred than as a perceived goal). This finding can be interpreted to indicate that the respondents value research but feel that it receives too much attention relative to other goals.

Another notable discrepancy between the perceived and the preferred goal structures is that certain adaptation goals are felt to receive too much emphasis. The goals of ensuring the confidence of financial contributors and of maintaining the favorable appraisal of validating bodies, in particular, occupy much lower positions on the preferred list than on the perceived list; the goals of keeping costs down and of satisfying area needs drop too, though less drastically. The position goal of maintaining or increasing prestige falls from second to eleventh place in the rankings. Apparently the time and energy that must be spent in winning external approval and in securing or bettering the university's reputation are resented by the busy administrator.

To obtain a more complete picture of the harmony or discord that exists at American universities, we compared the perceived and the preferred goal structures at particular institutions. In general, there is considerable congruence between the ideal and the actual and, by inference, a high degree of satisfaction among faculty and administrators that goals are receiving the proper emphasis. For example, at universities where the perceived goal of educating all legally qualified high school graduates has a high mean score relative to the score it receives at other universities or is ranked in the top third of all goals at the university, there is a commensurate tendency to give it a high rating or ranking as a preferred goal; the converse holds true at those institutions where the goal receives a low rating or ranking. In this case, we may conclude that a university's admissions policies make a considerable difference to its personnel. If that policy is inconsistent with a person's conception of what should be, then he will probably not be attracted to the university in the first place or will move on to a more congenial institution or perhaps alter his own goal values. The same conclusions hold true for roughly half of the 47 goals. With respect to the others, whatever discrepancies exist between what is and what ought to be are not serious or pervasive enough to create tension that would cause the faculty member or administrator to leave; or possibly, in these instances, he chooses to stay in the hopes of joining with others in changing the goal emphases through cooperative efforts.

GLOBAL CHARACTERISTICS AND GOAL STRUCTURES

It is often assumed that certain global characteristics of an institution are closely related to its policies and emphases. For example, we hear a great deal about the effects of size, with the big universities regarded as having certain qualities (most of them bad) that are absent at the smaller universities. Our analysis gives no confirmation to this particular bit of folklore. The larger universities in the sample pursue essentially the same goals as the smaller ones, whether bigness is measured by size of the student body or of the staff.

The region in which the university is located is another negligible characteristic, insofar as goal emphases and preferences are concerned. There are a few differences in the goals valued by persons at rural universities and those valued by persons at urban universities, but the findings are sparse.

The Elitist—"Service" Dichotomy

On the other hand, with respect to the global characteristics of productivity (as measured by number of doctorates awarded and by dollar volume of contract research), prestige (as measured by ratings of quality made by a nationwide sample of faculty and administrators), and graduate emphasis (as measured by the percentage of graduate students in the student body), a clear pattern of relationships emerges, and it is similar for all three measures. Those universities ranking high on any of these measures manifest an elitist pattern of perceived goals: They emphasize developing the student's intellective and scholarly qualities; they carry on pure research; they see themselves as centers for disseminating ideas and preserving the cultural heritage. With respect to support goals, they stress those aimed at satisfying the desires and needs of the faculty, they tend to slight undergraduate instruction but to encourage graduate work, and they demonstrate a concern for position goals having to do with the top quality of the academic program and with prestige.

Universities ranking low on these characteristics—i.e., those that are relatively unproductive, low in prestige, and lacking strong emphasis on graduate work—manifest a "service" orientation in their perceived goal structures: They give relatively great emphasis to such nonintellective student output goals as preparing the student for a useful career and cultivating his taste and to direct service and adaptation goals that involve giving the surrounding community practical help and maintaining the favor of outside agencies or groups. Each of the three global characteristics has its own peculiarities; the pattern is slightly different for each, but the basic antithesis is there in all three analyses.

So it is with the pattern of preferred goals, though here there is more variation among the three global characteristics. They have fewer goals in common, and the relationships tend to be negative: The goals are valued highly at universities ranking low on these global characteristics.

Comparing the perceived and preferred goal structures, we find no manifestations of outright dissonance that might indicate a state of tension and stress. For instance, although the intellective student goals and some of the position goals are emphasized at universities ranked high on these global characteristics, there is no particular feeling that they should be given precedence, but neither is there any tendency to rate them low on the preferred scale. The same is true for the goal of rewarding the faculty member for his contribution to his profession. At the more productive, prestigious, graduate-oriented universities, there *is* a tendency to feel that he should *not* be rewarded for his contribution to the institution, but no particular inclination either to emphasize or to subordinate this goal. In short, in no instance is a goal strongly emphasized but accorded very low value, and vice versa. This finding suggests again the selective nature of an American university, which seems to attract and hold those persons whose values accord with its particular goal emphases.

It has become a commonplace to assert that with the influx of Federal funds into higher education and the pressure on all universities to respond to society's needs, private and public universities have become virtually indistinguishable. But our findings with respect to yet another global characteristic—type of control —by no means support this assertion. On the contrary, they indicate clearly that strong differences still exist. The private university manifests an elitist pattern, being particularly concerned with the student's intellect, with motivation goals relating to faculty well-being, and with position goals relating to quality and prestige. State universities, on the other hand, are more inclined to give precedence (in both perceived and preferred goal structures) to developing qualities in the student other than the purely intellectual, to offering practical services to citizens, and to adapting to the demands of outside groups and agencies.

The strongest relationships occur for the two goals that concern admissions policies, with private universities emphasizing and assigning high value to the goal of accommodating only those students of high academic potential and state universities to the goal of educating to the utmost every high school graduate who meets the legal requirements for admission.

POWER-HOLDERS AND GOAL EMPHASES

The differences between private and public universities are both underscored and partly explained by the analyses that relate power structure to global characteristics. The influence of legislators and citizens makes itself felt much more strongly at state universities, of course, so it is hardly to be wondered at that these universities concern themselves with the goals that they do, particularly such goals as keeping costs down and providing services to citizens. At private universities, large private donors are among the more important power figures, and their dominance probably accounts for the stress laid on the goal of maintaining the confidence of contributors. Type of control was the global characteristic most closely related to power structure. Prestige, graduate emphasis, and location are also associated with power structure to some extent, but the findings here are fewer and not always easy to interpret.

Granting that the power of legislators, the Federal and state governments, large private donors, and citizens varies depending on whether a university is public or private, we find much less variation with respect to power structure than is commonly assumed. At almost all institutions in the sample, the president heads the list: He is perceived universally as having a great deal of say in the big decisions (mean score of 4.65 on a 5-point scale). Unhappily for the sake of our analyses, the president's power was virtually a constant, and thus no findings emerged about what effect a very strong (as distinct from a moderately strong) president has on goal structure.

Although some of them often regard themselves as relatively weak—mere rubber stamps—regents are perceived as having only slightly less power than the president. Perhaps our respondents were thinking here of their formal power rather than of the power they normally exercise. The vice-president ranks third in the power structure, and deans of professional schools, of graduate schools, and of liberal arts follow, in that order. Faculty and chairmen fall in the middle of the power structure, with faculty as a group regarded as having more power than chairmen as a group. At the bottom of the list are alumni, students, citizens, and parents, groups often assumed to exert a sinister influence on the university.

In short, it is clear that administrators are the people who make the big decisions in the university and that, in the eyes of our respondents, they have greater power than the faculty, whose power is by no means negligible (mean score of 3.31).

In the analyses of the relation between power structure and goals, there were almost no findings for some groups whose power is a constant and thus not amenable to our statistical manipulations. Such was the case for presidents, vice-presidents, and the four bottom-ranked groups. Findings were also sparse for deans of graduate schools.

One remarkable finding, in view of the alarm occasioned by increasing Federal involvement in higher education: Those universities where Federal agencies are perceived as having considerable influence do not differ markedly from those where the government has little say. There is some tendency for the former to subordinate the student intellective goals and the students' rights goals and to emphasize doing applied research, ensuring the confidence of contributors, and involving students in university government, but no other goals were found to be significant in this analysis.

With respect to regents—and here again, their power is virtually a constant—those few goals that proved to have significant relationships indicate that regents are little concerned with the student's intellectual development or rights and that they tend to denigrate giving faculty members maximum opportunity to pursue their careers. The goals to which they give precedence are keeping costs down and educating all legally qualified students. This somewhat anti-intellectual and practical bias is even more marked at universities where legislators or the state government has considerable influence.

"Outsiders" and Academics

The crucial point here is that, with respect to the relation between power structure and goal emphases, the dichotomy is not between administrators and faculty members: It is between the "outsiders" (legislators, the state government, regents—

who though technically within the university actually share little in its day-to-day life) and the academicians. Again, an antithesis between "service" and elitist goals emerges. At universities where deans of liberal arts and of professional schools, chairmen as a group, or the faculty have considerable power, the goals emphasized are output goals relating to intellect, pure research, and the university as a repository and generator of knowledge, and support goals relating to the faculty's participation in governance, professional well-being, and scholarly interests and to the institution's prestige and position. The patterns for the four groups contain minor variations, but these are slight. In short, our analyses give no support to the contention that administrators differ so much in outlook from faculty members that the goals they emphasize, when they have power, run counter to faculty interests.

Comparison of the backgrounds, perceived goals, and preferred goals of the two groups give further support to this assertion. Many of the differences between the two groups are attributable chiefly to the greater age of administrators. Others, such as the greater tendency for administrators to be Protestant, male, and white, apparently have little effect on their perceptions and attitudes as revealed in their goal structures: In only a few cases did faculty members disagree with administrators on what goals were emphasized, and the degree of disagreement was slight. More important, the same was true for preferred goals, a finding which suggests that faculty members have generally the same values as administrators and would not change the direction of the university even if they had greater power. Moreover, the same findings emerge when we compare administrators by rank; that is, higher ranking administrators tend to agree with faculty quite as much as do lower ranking administrators.

THE HIGHLIGHTS

In summary, the study indicates clearly that administrators and faculty tend to see eye to eye to a much greater extent than is commonly supposed and that therefore the greater power of administrators should not be regarded as necessarily inimical to the faculty or as inconsistent with the fundamental role and purposes of the university. It demonstrates, too, that clear differences among universities still exist, despite fears that our institutions of higher education are becoming more and more alike.

Throughout the analyses of global characteristics and of power structure, clear distinctions emerged between elitist goals and "service" goals, between universities which emphasized intellect, scholarship, faculty interests, and prestige and those which emphasized nonintellective student development, direct service to the community, and the satisfaction of outside constituencies. Finally, the high degree of congruence that exists between perceived and preferred goals at particular institutions underscores the selective nature of our universities, their tendency to attract and keep faculty and administrators who are in basic sympathy with the goal emphases of the university.

APPENDIX A
KEY TO ABBREVIATED FORMS OF GOAL ITEMS

APPENDIX B
ORGANIZATIONAL ANALYSIS
AND CALCULATION OF PRESTIGE SCORES

APPENDIX C
THE QUESTIONNAIRE

APPENDIX A

KEY TO ABBREVIATED FORMS OF GOAL ITEMS

OUTPUT GOALS:

Brief descriptions of the two major categories and the eight subcategories of goals will be found in Chapter 1, pp. 13–16.

Student-Expressive

1. Cultivate student's intellect

   Produce a student who, whatever else may be done to him, has had his intellect cultivated to the maximum.

2. Produce well-rounded student

   Produce a well-rounded student, that is, one whose physical, social, moral, intellectual, and esthetic potentialities have all been cultivated.

3. Affect student with great ideas

   Make sure the student is permanently affected (in mind and spirit) by the great ideas of the great minds of history.

4. Develop student's objectivity

   Assist students to develop objectivity about themselves and their beliefs and hence examine those beliefs critically.

5. Develop student's character

   Develop the inner character of students so that they can make sound, correct moral choices.

Student-Instrumental

6. Prepare students for useful careers

   Prepare students specifically for useful careers.

7. Prepare students for status/leadership

   Provide the student with skills, attitudes, contacts, and experiences which maximize the likelihood of his occupying a high status in life and a position of leadership in society.

118

8. Train students for scholarship/research

Train students in methods of scholarship and/or scientific research and/or creative endeavor.

9. Cultivate student's taste

Make a good consumer of the student—a person who is elevated culturally, has good taste, and can make good consumer choices.

10. Prepare student for citizenship

Produce a student who is able to perform his citizenship responsibilities effectively.

Research

11. Carry on pure research

Carry on pure research.

12. Carry on applied research

Carry on applied research.

Direct Service

13. Provide special adult training

Provide special training for part-time adult students, through extension courses, special short courses, correspondence courses, etc.

14. Assist citizens through extension programs

Assist citizens directly through extension programs, advice, consultation, and the provision of useful or needed facilities and services other than teaching.

15. Provide community cultural leadership

Provide cultural leadership for the community through university-sponsored programs in the arts, public lectures by distinguished persons, athletic events, and other performances, displays, or celebrations which present the best of culture, popular or not.

16. Disseminate new ideas

Serve as a center for the dissemination of new ideas that will change the society, whether those ideas are in science, literature, the arts, or politics.

17. Preserve cultural heritage

Serve as a center for the preservation of the cultural heritage.

SUPPORT GOALS:

Adaptation

18. Ensure confidence of contributors

Ensure the continued confidence and hence support of those who contribute substantially (other than students and recipients of services) to the finances and other material resource needs of the university.

19. Ensure favor of validating bodies

Ensure the favorable appraisal of those who validate the quality of the programs we offer (validating groups include accrediting bodies, professional societies, scholarly peers at other universities, and respected persons in intellectual or artistic circles).

20. Educate to utmost high school graduates

Educate to his utmost capacities every high school graduate who meets basic legal requirements for admission.

21. Accept good students only

Accommodate only students of high potential in terms of the specific strengths and emphases of this university.

22. Satisfy area needs

Orient ourselves to the satisfaction of the special needs and problems of the immediate geographical region.

23. Keep costs down

Keep costs down as low as possible, through more efficient utilization of time and space, reduction of course duplication, etc.

24. Hold staff in face of inducements

Hold our staff in the face of inducements offered by other universities.

Management

25. Reward for contribution to profession

Make sure that salaries, teaching assignments, perquisites, and privileges always reflect the contribution that the person involved is making to his own profession or discipline.

26. Involve faculty in university government

Involve faculty in the government of the university.

27. Involve students in university government

Involve students in the government of the university.

28. Run university democratically

Make sure the university is run democratically insofar as that is feasible.

29. Keep harmony

Keep harmony between departments or divisions of the university when such departments or divisions do not see eye to eye on important matters.

30. Reward for contribution to institution

Make sure that salaries, teaching assignments, perquisites, and privileges always reflect the contribution that the person involved is making to the functioning of this university.

31. Emphasize undergraduate instruction

Emphasize undergraduate instruction even at the expense of the graduate program.

32. Encourage graduate work

Encourage students to go into graduate work.

33. Ensure efficient goal attainment

Make sure the university is run by those selected according to their ability to attain the goals of the university in the most efficient manner possible.

34. Let will of faculty prevail

Make sure that on *all* important issues (not only curriculum), the will of the full-time faculty shall prevail.

Motivation

35. Protect academic freedom

Protect the faculty's right to academic freedom.

36. Give faculty maximum opportunity to pursue careers

Make this a place in which faculty have maximum opportunity to pursue their careers in a manner satisfactory to them by their own criteria.

37. Provide student activities

Provide a full round of student activities.

38. Protect students' right of inquiry

Protect and facilitate the students' right to inquire into, investigate, and examine critically any idea or program that they might get interested in.

39. Protect students' right of action

Protect and facilitate the students' right to advocate direct action of a political or social kind and any attempts on their part to organize efforts to attain political or social goals.

40. Develop faculty loyalty to institution

Develop loyalty on the part of the faculty and staff to the university, rather than only to their own jobs or professional concerns.

41. Develop pride in university

Develop greater pride on the part of faculty, staff, and students in their university and the things it stands for.

Position

42. Maintain top quality in all programs

Maintain top quality in all programs we engage in.

43. Maintain top quality in important programs

Maintain top quality in those programs we feel to be especially important (other programs being, of course, up to acceptable standards).

44. Maintain balanced quality in all programs

Maintain a balanced level of quality across the whole range of programs we engage in.

45. Keep up to date

Keep up to date and responsive.

46. Increase or maintain prestige

Increase the prestige of the university or, if you believe it is already extremely high, ensure the maintenance of that prestige.

47. Preserve institutional character

Keep this place from becoming something different from what it is now; that is, preserve its peculiar emphases and point of view, its "character."

APPENDIX B

ORGANIZATIONAL ANALYSIS AND CALCULATION
OF PRESTIGE SCORES

A detailed account of the methods employed in calculating organizational scores for the goals and power measures is given here. The procedures used to determine the prestige level of universities are also described.

CALCULATION OF ORGANIZATIONAL SCORES

Two fundamental kinds of analyses were used: individual and organizational. The individual analysis is one in which some attribute of a person is related to some other attribute—e.g., the attribute of position (administrator or faculty member) and the attribute of social class origin. One may ask, for example, whether administrators come from a higher socioeconomic class than do faculty members. The organizational analysis is one in which the university itself is conceived of as a single individual. We may therefore deal with two attributes of the university —e.g., size and location—to see how they relate to one another. (Do universities in the East tend to be larger than universities in the West?) The greater part of our analysis and discussion deals with organizational relationships, chiefly because one of the outstanding characteristics of the study is the large number of institutions that it includes—considerably more than do most organizational studies. The measures employed usually involve single figures (percentages and means, for instance) or rank orderings of variables.

To clarify the concept of an organizational relationship, we paraphrase a portion of the instructions to the research and programming staff concerning the calculation of our major measures.

ORGANIZATIONAL RELATIONSHIPS

In an "organizational relationship," the university is conceived of as a single individual. Measures are single figures such as means, percentages, or ranks which characterize the university as a whole. An example is size of university, as measured by number of full-time faculty members, or the prestige of the university, as measured on a five-point scale. For example, one hypothesis about organizational relationship might be the following: the more prestigious the university, the larger the university.

124

A good many of the organizational variables are averages drawn from the questionnaire. For example, question 2.1 asks the respondent to indicate who he thinks "make the big decisions" at his university. He is to check the appropriate spaces, as shown below:

	a great deal of say	quite a bit of say	some say	very little say	no say at all
The regents (or trustees)..	____	____	____	____	____
Legislators...............	____	____	____	____	____
Sources of large private grants or endowments..	____	____	____	____	____
Federal government offices or agencies...........	____	____	____	____	____
etc.					

At a given university, the average score may be used to characterize the power of the indicated persons or groups at that university. We present, for example, the replies dealing with "The regents (or trustees)" for two major universities.

	a great deal of say	quite a bit of say	some say	very little say	no say at all
University X...........	46	40	30	5	1
University Y...........	148	45	8	2	1

As is clear, both universities show skewed distributions, since we find that regents tend to be highly rated everywhere. Nevertheless, the comparative differences are large. The weighted arithmetic mean is to be calculated in each case by assigning a weight of 5 for "a great deal of say," 4 for "quite a bit of say," 3 for "some say," and so forth. The results in this case are:

| University X | 4.02 |
| University Y | 4.67 |

The measures are to be calculated for all universities, and the scores are to be ranged in order from lowest to highest. The distribution is then to be divided into thirds. The thirds will be called "high," "medium," and "low." Since University X's score falls in the lower third, we will say that the power of the regents there is "low." Since University Y's score falls in the top third, we will say that the power of the regents there is "high."

In this way, we will obtain a score for all 68 universities which will enable us to rate a university as high, medium, or low on the power of the regents. We will then relate the power of regents to some other university characteristic—for example, size. As explained in Chapter 1, we use Goodman and Kruskal's *gamma* as our measure of the size of the relationship and use a modified form of the "z" measure which they suggest as a test of significance.

When we use the number of full-time staff as our measure of size of university, the results are as shown in the following table:

| | | Size of Institution | | | |
		Small	Medium	Large	Total
	High	10	8	5	23
Power of	Medium	8	6	8	22
Regents	Low	5	8	10	23
	Total	23	22	23	68

$Gamma = -0.283$ $z = -1.156$

We made use of the 5 percent level of significance, requiring a z of 1.96 or higher. As will be seen, we only report findings (with the obtained *gammas*) when the findings are significant. Hence the above finding is not reported in the text.

The above table suggests that there is a slight negative relationship between size and power of regents. That is, as the size of the university increases, the power of the regents goes down (or at least, is perceived to go down). The z, being below 1.96, suggests that this value of *gamma* could come up by chance a good deal more often than five times in a hundred. (About 25 times in 100.) (Contrary to the belief of many who blame the size of the university for its troubles, we found that size was associated with very few of the characteristics of the university that we investigated.)

The following measures were calculated for each university:

Goal Measure 1 (GM 1)

This measure is derived from a ranking of the weighted means of "perceived goal" responses. For HOLD OUR STAFF, at University Z, we get:

Absolute	Great	Med	Little	None	Total
5	55	51	11	2	124

If we set scores of "4" for Absolute, "3" for Great, etc., then the weighted mean comes to 2.3. The standard deviation for this mean comes to a trifle over 1.0. We set a rule that the standard deviation must not exceed 1.5. If it does, we call the goal "confused," and so treat it from then on. In this case, the goal is not confused, so we may use the weighted mean as a measure of its importance. We then calculated the weighted mean for HOLD OUR STAFF at each of the 68 universities. Then we range the means in sequence from the lowest to the highest, cut the distribution in approximately three equal parts, call the top group "high," the next "medium," and the bottom group "low." In the case of this university, the weighted mean of 2.3 fell in the "medium" category. This, then, is Goal Measure 1 for Hold Our Staff at University Z. In all calculations involving Hold Our Staff, Goal Measure 1 for University Z is "medium."

Goal Measure 2 (GM 2)

We use the weighted mean, as in GM 1. In this case, we draw up a distribution of *all* the perceived goal means at University Z. For Hold Our Staff, the mean is 2.3; for Will of Faculty, the mean is 1.9; etc., split into thirds. Perhaps the mean of 2.3 now falls into the "high" category at University Z. This goal (Hold Our Staff) is now called "high," and is Goal Measure 2 for this goal.

Certain other goal measures were also calculated but are not reported on here. The two described above make up what we came to call the "across-universities" and "within-university" measure of goal emphasis, respectively. We performed a similar analysis for preferred goals (that is, replies to the portion of the first question that respondents made to the Should Be line on the goal questions).

The power structure measures were calculated in corresponding fashion. The instructions to our research staff for the two relevant measures were:

Power Structure Measure 1 (PSM 1)

Calculated in a manner similar to GM 1. For Decide Regents the data for University Z are:

Great	69
Quite a Bit	42
Some	13
Little	1
None	0

If we weight Great, 4, Quite a Bit, 3, etc., then the weighted mean is 3.4. Range all 68 universities in sequence, split weighted mean distribution into thirds, call them high, medium, and low. This is PSM 1 for regents. Perform similar operations to obtain PSM 1 scores for legislators, sources of large private grants or endowments, etc.

Power Structure Measure 2 (PSM 2)

Calculated in a manner similar to Goal Measure 2. Here the weighted means for each power group (regents, legislators, etc.) at a given university are ranged in order at the university. Split into thirds, called low, medium, and high. Then the university is characterized as one in which regents are rated high in power in comparison to other power-holders at that same university.

The above represent examples of scores which are weighted by response rate. As noted in the report, a variety of different weightings were employed, with relatively little difference in results. In any case, it is arguable whether one should make the arbitrary determination that, for example, all universities should count equally, irrespective of size or other organizational characteristics. Similarly, within the university, we tried various weighting schemes, such as that in which we assigned equal weight to higher administrators, dean-level administrators, chairmen, and faculty. We then calculated a university score which was the arithmetic mean of those four means. Again, some might question whether this weighting scheme is any more justifiable than one which is a simple arithmetic mean of all respondents. For example, on goal perceptions, is not one man's "view" as valid as any other man's? Or, to state it another way, why weight the view of the provost any more than the view of an assistant professor of English? Is not one man's perception as accurate, for him, as the other's?

PRESTIGE OF UNIVERSITIES

The prestige measure used in this study is based on Allan Cartter's *An Assessment of Quality in Graduate Education*,[1] a survey of the opinions of a nationwide sample of persons in university arts and sciences departments and engineering departments which give the Ph.D. Respondents were asked to rate the departments of other universities as "distinguished," "strong," "good," "adequate," "marginal," or "not sufficient to provide acceptable doctoral training." Departments were then ranked on the basis of their average scores. Although Cartter calculated averages for disciplinary areas, such as the social sciences and humanities, within the university, he did not attempt to secure averages for the university as a whole. His reason was a good one: Universities differ in the number of departments rated. The largest universities have as many as 29 departments which give the Ph.D., whereas institutions like M.I.T. and Caltech, because of their specialized character, have a very small number of departments. Thus it is possible for such institutions to attain a high over-all average relative to more heterogeneous universities, simply because they do not offer work in as many areas.

For our purposes, however, an average measure for the university was necessary. Because universities are not identified by name in this study, and because they are classified into only four prestige levels, the dangers of using an over-all average seemed slight. We therefore followed

[1] Washington: American Council on Education, 1966.

the Cartter procedure, supplementing the information contained in his study with extra information, provided by Dr. Cartter, on those universities whose ranks he does not report. In addition, we developed measures which took into account the number of departments at a university.

The procedure utilized the following principles.

(1) A university might have as many as 29 rated departments, e.g., anthropology, economics, physiology. It was not necessary for any set number to have been evaluated (i.e., University A, 10 departments; University B, 5 departments; University C, 2 departments).

(2) The evaluation of the departments ranged from I–VI (one highest–six lowest). On the basis of quantities assigned to given ranks, the evaluation of the departments ranged from 4+ to 3 for the top scores. A mean score was assigned to those evaluated as IV, V, or VI.

$$IV = 2.75$$
$$V = 2.25$$
$$VI = 1.75$$

Those rated I, II, or III were given the mean value actually obtained.

(3) *Scores*

Score I: The *number* of departments rated for each university was counted to obtain total number of departments rated as well as number rated IV, V, or VI. A *weighted sum* was obtained by adding the sums appropriate to a given ranking. A *weighted mean* for each university was obtained by dividing the weighted sum of each university by the number of departments rated for that university. This *weighted mean* constituted score I.

Score II: The weighted mean (score I) for each school plus the weighted sum for each school constituted score II.

Score III: The weighted mean (score I) plus the number of departments rated for each school constituted score III.

(4) The scores I, II, and III were ordered separately in descending order. This comprised three scores for each university. (Data for two universities in our sample, Auburn and Georgia, were not available.)

(5) The top ten scores for Score I, II, and III were assigned a 1, the next ten, a 2; the next 22, a 3; and those remaining were assigned a 4. The number of institutions in each level as given by Berelson minus the schools not included in our sample was used to determine the number of universities assigned a 1, 2, 3, or 4 level on a given score.

(Text continues on page 132.)

EXAMPLE OF PRESTIGE CALCULATION

	Anthro	Hist	Psych	Eng	Chem	Geology	Bacteriology	Biochem	Botany	Entem	Pharmacol	Physio	Zoo	Phys
Univ. A	4.59 IV	3.76	4.88						3.52					3.39
Univ. B	2.75					V 2.25	4.00					3.76	3.51	
Univ. C		VI 1.75		VI 1.75							IV 2.75	V 2.25		
Univ. D	VI 1.75						VI 1.75			VI 1.75				

UNIVERSITY A

N*	Scores
1	4.59
1	3.52
1	4.88
1	3.39
1	3.76
5	20.14

4.03

UNIVERSITY B

N	Scores
1	2.75
1	3.76
1	2.25
1	4.00
1	3.51
5	16.27

3.25

UNIVERSITY C

N	Scores
1	1.75
1	1.75
1	2.25
1	2.75
4	8.50

2.13

UNIVERSITY D

N	Scores
1	1.75
1	1.75
1	1.75
3	5.25

1.75

$$\text{Score I} = \frac{\text{weighted sum}}{N}$$

Score II = weighted sum + weighted mean

$$
\begin{array}{ll}
20.14 & 16.27 \quad\quad 8.50 \\
\underline{4.03} & \underline{3.25} \quad\quad \underline{2.13} \\
24.17 & 19.52 \quad\quad 10.63
\end{array}
$$

Score III = weighted mean + N

$$
\begin{array}{ll}
4.03 & 3.25 \quad\quad 2.13 \\
\underline{5} & \underline{5} \quad\quad\quad \underline{4} \\
9.03 & 8.25 \quad\quad 6.13
\end{array}
$$

$$
\begin{array}{l}
1.75 \\
\underline{5.25} \\
7.00
\end{array}
\qquad
\begin{array}{l}
1.75 \\
\underline{3} \\
4.75
\end{array}
$$

	Score I		Score II		Score III		Level
(A)	4.03	(A)	24.17	(A)	9.03		1
(B)	3.25	(B)	19.52	(B)	8.25		2
(C)	2.13	(C)	10.63	(C)	6.13		3
(D)	1.75	(D)	7.00	(D)	4.75		4

*N = number of departments

(6) The three scores of a given university obtained in (5) above were averaged. This average was the prestige level to which a given school was assigned. (A ⅓ fraction was rounded up, a ⅔ fraction was rounded down—1⅓=1; 1⅔=2.) Auburn and Georgia were assigned to level 4.

(7) Not all universities averaged perfectly, and rounding was necessary. As it turned out, the university with two scores in the same level and one in a different level ended up with the majority score as the prestige level to which it was assigned. In only two cases did a university have an average based on scores from three different levels.

APPENDIX C

The Questionnaire

ACADEMIC ADMINISTRATORS AND UNIVERSITY GOALS

A STUDY OF THE

CENTER FOR ACADEMIC ADMINISTRATION RESEARCH

UNIVERSITY OF MINNESOTA

EDWARD GROSS

PROFESSOR OF SOCIOLOGY

and

PAUL V. GRAMBSCH

DEAN, SCHOOL OF BUSINESS ADMINISTRATION

and

PROFESSOR OF MANAGEMENT

This questionnaire is being given to *all* presidents, vice-presidents, deans, department chairmen and a carefully selected sample of other academic administrators and of nonadmnistrative faculty at 80 major universities in the United States. A study of such scope has never before been attempted. It will provide us with a comprehensive picture of who administrators are, how they see the university, and how they differ in their influence on university policy. In spite of the magnitude of the study it depends completely on the kindness and generosity of each respondent. The results should be of value to you in your university work. They will appear in the form of published articles and monographs.

This research is supported by the UNITED STATES OFFICE OF EDUCATION.

133

This questionnaire is completely confidential. No one will see it except the professional members of our research staff. Nevertheless, for purposes of control of returns, we need your name to serve as a double-check on the accuracy of our number control system. We can then check it off our sample list so that we know who has been heard from. Please write it in here:

NAME

1. THE GOALS OF THIS UNIVERSITY

One of the great issues in American education has to do with the proper aims or goals of the university. The question is: What are we trying to accomplish? Are we trying to prepare people for jobs, to broaden them intellectually, or what? Below we have listed a large number of the more commonly claimed aims, intentions or goals of a university. We would like you to react to each of these in two different ways:

(1) How important *is* each aim at this university?

(2) How important *should* the aim be at this university?

	of absolutely top importance	of great importance	of medium importance	of little importance	of no importance	don't know or can't say
EXAMPLE:						
to serve as substitute parents	**is** ☐	☐	☒	☐	☐	☐
	should be ☐	☐	☐	☐	☒	☐

A person who had checked the alternatives in the manner shown above would be expressing his perception that the aim, intention or goal, "to serve as substitute parents," *is* of medium importance at his university but that he believes it *should be of no importance* as an aim, intention, or goal of his university.

NOTE: "of absolutely top importance" should only be checked if the aim is *so* important that, if it were to be removed, the university would be shaken to its very roots and its character changed in a fundamental way.

ALL QUESTIONS ARE ABOUT *THIS* UNIVERSITY, that is, THE ONE AT WHICH YOU ARE PRESENTLY EMPLOYED.

GOALS

		of absolutely top importance	of great importance	of medium importance	of little importance	of no importance	don't know or can't say
hold our staff in the face of inducements offered by other universities	is	☐	☐	☐	☐	☐	☐
	should be	☐	☐	☐	☐	☐	☐
make sure that on *all* important issues (not only curriculum), the will of the full-time faculty shall prevail	is	☐	☐	☐	☐	☐	☐
	should be	☐	☐	☐	☐	☐	☐
encourage students to go into graduate work	is	☐	☐	☐	☐	☐	☐
	should be	☐	☐	☐	☐	☐	☐
protect the faculty's right to academic freedom	is	☐	☐	☐	☐	☐	☐
	should be	☐	☐	☐	☐	☐	☐
provide special training for part-time adult students, through extension courses, special short courses, correspondence courses, etc.	is	☐	☐	☐	☐	☐	☐
	should be	☐	☐	☐	☐	☐	☐

GOALS (cont.)

	of absolutely top importance	of great importance	of medium importance	of little importance	of no importance	don't know or can't say
develop loyalty on the part of the faculty and staff to the university, rather than only to their own jobs or professional concerns — **is**	☐	☐	☐	☐	☐	☐
should be	☐	☐	☐	☐	☐	☐
produce a student who, whatever else may be done to him, has had his intellect cultivated to the maximum — **is**	☐	☐	☐	☐	☐	☐
should be	☐	☐	☐	☐	☐	☐
develop the inner character of students so that they can make sound, correct moral choices — **is**	☐	☐	☐	☐	☐	☐
should be	☐	☐	☐	☐	☐	☐
make a good consumer of the student—a person who is elevated culturally, has good taste, and can make good consumer choices — **is**	☐	☐	☐	☐	☐	☐
should be	☐	☐	☐	☐	☐	☐
serve as a center for the dissemination of new ideas that will change the society, whether those ideas are in science, literature, the arts, or politics — **is**	☐	☐	☐	☐	☐	☐
should be	☐	☐	☐	☐	☐	☐

is
should be

educate to his utmost capacities every high school graduate who meets basic legal requirements for admission

is
should be

keep harmony between departments or divisions of the university when such departments or divisions do not see eye to eye on important matters

is
should be

make this a place in which faculty have maximum opportunity to pursue their careers in a manner satisfactory to them by their own criteria

is
should be

develop greater pride on the part of faculty, staff and students in their university and the things it stands for

is
should be

keep up to date and responsive

is
should be

make sure the student is permanently affected (in mind and spirit) by the great ideas of the great minds of history

GOALS (cont.)

		of absolutely top importance	of great importance	of medium importance	of little importance	of no importance	don't know or can't say
train students in methods of scholarship and/or scientific research, and/or creative endeavor	is	☐	☐	☐	☐	☐	☐
	should be	☐	☐	☐	☐	☐	☐
serve as a center for the preservation of the cultural heritage	is	☐	☐	☐	☐	☐	☐
	should be	☐	☐	☐	☐	☐	☐
orient ourselves to the satisfaction of the special needs and problems of the immediate geographical region	is	☐	☐	☐	☐	☐	☐
	should be	☐	☐	☐	☐	☐	☐
involve students in the government of the university	is	☐	☐	☐	☐	☐	☐
	should be	☐	☐	☐	☐	☐	☐
make sure the university is run by those selected according to their ability to attain the goals of the university in the most efficient manner possible.	is	☐	☐	☐	☐	☐	☐
	should be	☐	☐	☐	☐	☐	☐
maintain top quality in all programs we engage in	is	☐	☐	☐	☐	☐	☐
	should be	☐	☐	☐	☐	☐	☐

□ □   □ □   □ □   □ □   □ □   □ □

□ □   □ □   □ □   □ □   □ □   □ □

□ □   □ □   □ □   □ □   □ □   □ □

□ □   □ □   □ □   □ □   □ □   □ □

□ □   □ □   □ □   □ □   □ □   □ □

□ □   □ □   □ □   □ □   □ □   □ □

is / **should be** — keep this place from becoming something different from what it is now; that is, preserve its peculiar emphases and point of view, its "character"

is / **should be** — provide the student with skills, attitudes, contacts, and experiences which maximize the likelihood of his occupying a high status in life and a position of leadership in society

is / **should be** — carry on pure research

is / **should be** — keep costs down as low as possible through more efficient utilization of time and space, reduction of course duplication, etc.

is / **should be** — make sure that salaries, teaching assignments, perquisites, and privileges always reflect the contribution that the person involved is making to the functioning of this university

is / **should be** — protect and facilitate the students' right to advocate direct action of a political or social kind, and any attempts on their part to organize efforts to attain political or social goals

GOALS (cont.)

	of absolutely top importance	of great importance	of medium importance	of little importance	of no importance	don't know or can't say
produce a well-rounded student, that is one whose physical, social, moral, intellectual and esthetic potentialities have all been cultivated						
is	☐	☐	☐	☐	☐	☐
should be	☐	☐	☐	☐	☐	☐
assist citizens directly through extension programs, advice, consultation, and the provision of useful or needed facilities and services other than through teaching						
is	☐	☐	☐	☐	☐	☐
should be	☐	☐	☐	☐	☐	☐
ensure the favorable appraisal of those who validate the quality of the programs we offer (validating groups include accrediting bodies, professional societies, scholarly peers at other universities, and respected persons in intellectual or artistic circles)						
is	☐	☐	☐	☐	☐	☐
should be	☐	☐	☐	☐	☐	☐
maintain a balanced level of quality across the whole range of programs we engage in						
is	☐	☐	☐	☐	☐	☐
should be	☐	☐	☐	☐	☐	☐
make sure the university is run democratically insofar as that is feasible						
is	☐	☐	☐	☐	☐	☐
should be	☐	☐	☐	☐	☐	☐

☐ ☐   ☐ ☐   ☐ ☐   ☐ ☐   ☐ ☐   ☐ ☐

☐ ☐   ☐ ☐   ☐ ☐   ☐ ☐   ☐ ☐   ☐ ☐

☐ ☐   ☐ ☐   ☐ ☐   ☐ ☐   ☐ ☐   ☐ ☐

☐ ☐   ☐ ☐   ☐ ☐   ☐ ☐   ☐ ☐   ☐ ☐

☐ ☐   ☐ ☐   ☐ ☐   ☐ ☐   ☐ ☐   ☐ ☐

☐ ☐   ☐ ☐   ☐ ☐   ☐ ☐   ☐ ☐   ☐ ☐

is / **should be** — produce a student who is able to perform his citizenship responsibilities effectively

is / **should be** — accommodate only students of high potential in terms of the specific strengths and emphases of this university

is / **should be** — assist students to develop objectivity about themselves and their beliefs and hence examine those beliefs critically

is / **should be** — prepare students specifically for useful careers

is / **should be** — provide cultural leadership for the community through university-sponsored programs in the arts, public lectures by distinguished persons, athletic events, and other performances, displays or celebrations which present the best of culture, popular or not

is / **should be** — carry on applied research

GOALS (cont.)

		of absolutely top importance	of great importance	of medium importance	of little importance	of no importance	don't know or can't say
ensure the continued confidence and hence support of those who contribute substantially (other than students and recipients of services) to the finances and other material resource needs of the university	is	☐	☐	☐	☐	☐	☐
	should be	☐	☐	☐	☐	☐	☐
make sure that salaries, teaching assignments, perquisites, and privileges always reflect the contribution that the person involved is making to *his own profession or discipline*	is	☐	☐	☐	☐	☐	☐
	should be	☐	☐	☐	☐	☐	☐
emphasize undergraduate instruction even at the expense of the graduate program	is	☐	☐	☐	☐	☐	☐
	should be	☐	☐	☐	☐	☐	☐
involve faculty in the government of the university	is	☐	☐	☐	☐	☐	☐
	should be	☐	☐	☐	☐	☐	☐
provide a full round of student activities	is	☐	☐	☐	☐	☐	☐
	should be	☐	☐	☐	☐	☐	☐
increase the prestige of the university or, if you believe it is already extremely high, ensure maintenance of that prestige	is	☐	☐	☐	☐	☐	☐
	should be	☐	☐	☐	☐	☐	☐

protect and facilitate the students' right to inquire into, investigate, and examine critically any idea or program that they might get interested in

is ☐ ☐ ☐ ☐ ☐ ☐

should be ☐ ☐ ☐ ☐ ☐ ☐

maintain top quality in those programs we feel to be especially important (other programs being, of course, up to acceptable standards)

is ☐ ☐ ☐ ☐ ☐ ☐

should be ☐ ☐ ☐ ☐ ☐ ☐

In spite of the length of the above list, it is entirely possible that we have not included aims or goals which are important at this university, or we may have badly stated such an aim or goal; if so, please take this opportunity to correct us by writing them in below.

GOAL		of absolutely top importance	of great importance	of medium importance	of little importance	of no importance	don't know or can't say
_____	**is**	☐	☐	☐	☐	☐	☐
	should be	☐	☐	☐	☐	☐	☐
_____	**is**	☐	☐	☐	☐	☐	☐
	should be	☐	☐	☐	☐	☐	☐

2. WHO MAKE THE BIG DECISIONS

2.1 Think again of the kind of place this university is; that is, what its major goals or distinctive emphases are. Below are listed a number of positions and agencies. In each case, indicate by a check mark in the appropriate space *how much say* you believe persons in those positions have in affecting the major goals of the university. Note we are asking only about the *university as a whole*. A man might have a lot of say in his own department, but not in the university as a whole.

	a great deal of say	quite a bit of say	some say	very little say	no say at all
The regents (or trustees)	☐	☐	☐	☐	☐
Legislators	☐	☐	☐	☐	☐
Sources of large private grants or endowments	☐	☐	☐	☐	☐
Federal government agencies or offices	☐	☐	☐	☐	☐
State government agencies or offices	☐	☐	☐	☐	☐
The President	☐	☐	☐	☐	☐
The vice-presidents (or provosts)	☐	☐	☐	☐	☐
Dean of the graduate school	☐	☐	☐	☐	☐
Dean of liberal arts	☐	☐	☐	☐	☐
Deans of professional schools as a group	☐	☐	☐	☐	☐
Chairmen of departments, considered as a group	☐	☐	☐	☐	☐
The faculty, as a group	☐	☐	☐	☐	☐
The students, as a group	☐	☐	☐	☐	☐
Parents of students, as a group	☐	☐	☐	☐	☐
The citizens of the state, as a group	☐	☐	☐	☐	☐
Alumni, as a group	☐	☐	☐	☐	☐

2.2   Below is listed a number of areas in which decisions of importance to the university must be made. How big a role would you say the faculty plays in each of those areas of decision-making? We are asking here for your total assessment, including not only formal participation (committees and the like) but informal influence, veto power, and any other kind of influence.

AREA OF DECISIONS	faculty views prevail completely	faculty have much influence	faculty have moderate influence	faculty have little influence
Educational policies	☐	☐	☐	☐
Faculty personnel policies	☐	☐	☐	☐
Financial affairs and capital improvements	☐	☐	☐	☐
Student affairs	☐	☐	☐	☐
Public and alumni relations	☐	☐	☐	☐

2.3   Each of the following external groups or agencies affect university operations in various ways. Some are viewed as desirable, some as not. What we would like to know is whether any or all of these groups or agencies affect the work *you* do in any ways that you can perceive.

	a major effect on my work	a moderate effect on my work	little effect on my work
Alumni of the university	☐	☐	☐
Agencies supplying funds for contract research	☐	☐	☐
local government	☐	☐	☐
state government (executive)	☐	☐	☐
state government (legislative)	☐	☐	☐

	a major effect on my work	a moderate effect on my work	little effect on my work
federal government	☐	☐	☐
accrediting bodies	☐	☐	☐
donors	☐	☐	☐
foundations	☐	☐	☐
churches or religious orders		☐	☐

3. ABOUT THE UNIVERSITY IN GENERAL

In general, how would you describe the rule-atmosphere at this university: (Please check the appropriate space)

☐ 1. I find it hard to believe there are *any* rules at all around here. People seem to do as they please.

☐ 2. In general, a good deal of laxity is permitted compared to what I know of other places.

☐ 3. The rules are respected, though exceptions are permitted when proper.

☐ 4. The rules are very important. Exceptions are very rare.

☐ 5. This is really a rule-emphasizing place, practically everything goes "by the book."

4. THE PERSON TO WHOM YOU GO FOR AN AUTHORITATIVE DECISION

Think now of the person to whom you regularly go when you need an authoritative decision on some line of action you contemplate in your work. (For a non-administrative faculty member, this would normally be the head of his department or section; for a chairman or head, the person would be his dean or director; for a dean or director, a vice-president or provost; for the president, the governing body as a group.)

Just so it is clear, please state the title of this person in your case: _____

4.1   How important would you say that person is in terms of your ability to do your job well:

☐ 1. Absolutely essential. Without his active cooperation and help, I could hardly operate at all.

☐ 2. Absolutely essential, but only in a veto sense. That is, if he blocks me, I am stymied.

☐ 3. Very important. He can make my job quite a lot easier, or quite a lot harder.

☐ 4. Important. He can make my job easier or harder.

☐ 5. Of only moderate importance. He is an obstacle who can give me trouble if he makes up his mind to but, much of the time, I do my job without much help or hindrance from him.

☐ 6. Of little significance to me in comparison with some others (for example, people in the community, or people at other universities).

4.2   Which of the following words come closest to describing that person's style of leadership?

☐ autocratic

☐ democratic

☐ laissez-faire (lets people do pretty well what they wish)

4.3   All things considered, how do you feel about your relationship to that person?

☐ 1. Completely satisfied

☐ 2. A good relationship on the whole, but there are some features of it I do not like.

☐ 3. Quite a few problems in dealing with him, but it could be worse.

☐ 4. A rather poor relationship, but I can live with it.

☐ 5. Completely unsatisfied.

4.4   How much autonomy do you feel you have in relation to that person:

   ☐ 1. Not enough

   ☐ 2. Just about the right amount

   ☐ 3. Too much

4.5   How close are you to him socially? (Please check an appropriate space)

Very close._____|_____|_____|_____|_____ Strictly business

5. THE POWER I HAVE

On the line below indicate with a check the approximate amount of power you feel you have to get the things done that you would like to get done in connection with your university role.

A great deal _____|_____|_____|_____ No power at all

6. CRITERIA OF EVALUATION

Periodically department chairmen and deans are faced with the task of evaluating members of the faculty for purposes of recommending salary increments and promotions. Granting, with Tawney, that a man's "worth is something between his God and himself," what criteria do you think administrators should use in evaluating faculty members?

Below are listed some of the more commonly mentioned criteria. Indicate in the appropriate bracket your view of how important they should be.

	very important	important	of little importance
Teaching performance	☐	☐	☐
Publications	☐	☐	☐
Honors received	☐	☐	☐

Student evaluations

Other job offers received

Service to the community

Total effectiveness in working with students

Ability to secure research grants

Statements of other faculty members

Ability to get along with colleagues

Research accomplished

Research potential

Committee and other administrative service

OTHER IMPORTANT CRITERIA

_____

_____

_____

7.1   Below is listed a number of the major schools and colleges in this university. We would like you to indicate your ranking of each one in terms of the *calibre of the faculty*, as you believe it to be. In most cases, presumably, only two or three should be ranked as falling in the first category: "calibre at the very top." The basis of comparison should be limited to this university only. Thus "calibre at the very top" means at the very top *here*, not at *all* universities. If you have no such school, just leave it blank.

	calibre at the very top	first-rate faculty—but some exceptions	a good calibre group, but needs some improvement	faculty comes up to minimal standards only	too many of faculty are below par. A source of embarrassment
Engineering	□	□	□	□	□
Dentistry	□	□	□	□	□
Education	□	□	□	□	□
Pharmacy	□	□	□	□	□
Law	□	□	□	□	□
Architecture	□	□	□	□	□
Medicine	□	□	□	□	□
Veterinary Medicine	□	□	□	□	□
Social Sciences	□	□	□	□	□
Physical Sciences	□	□	□	□	□
Humanities	□	□	□	□	□
Business School	□	□	□	□	□
Home Economics	□	□	□	□	□
Agriculture	□	□	□	□	□
Forestry	□	□	□	□	□
Journalism	□	□	□	□	□
Social Work	□	□	□	□	□
Nursing	□	□	□	□	□
Public Health	□	□	□	□	□

7.2 Which of the following comes closer to your conception of the proper posture for an academic dean to assume in his relations with the higher university administration: (If you yourself are an academic dean, then answer this question in terms of yourself only. If you are a department chairman, answer this question in terms of the dean who heads your division or school.)

☐ (a) *Primarily* a representative of his area of responsibility *to* the university administration.

☐ (b) *Primarily* a representative of the university administration *to* his area of responsibility.

7.3 Which of the following comes closer to your conception of the proper posture for a department chairman to assume in his relations with his dean: (If you yourself are an academic dean, answer this only in terms of the department chairmen who report to you. If you are a chairman, answer the question only in terms of your relations with your own dean.)

☐ (a) *Primarily* a representative of his department *to* the dean.

☐ (b) *Primarily* a representative of his dean *to* his department.

8. SOME OF YOUR IDEAS ABOUT YOURSELF AND YOUR WORK

8.1 It would take some very strong inducements to get me to leave this university for a position elsewhere.

strongly agree	agree	undecided	disagree	strongly disagree
☐	☐	☐	☐	☐

8.2 Would you leave this university if you were offered a job at one of the top five (in excellence or quality) universities in the country? (If you yourself feel you are now in one of the top five, then think of one of the other four):

☐ At a substantially lower salary

☐ At the same salary

☐ At a substantially higher salary

☐ Wouldn't leave

8.3 I get most of my intellectual stimulation from: (please number in rank order, with 1 meaning most stimulation and 4 least stimulation)

☐ On-campus colleagues and associates

☐ Professional associates elsewhere

☐ Periodicals, books, and other publications

☐ Groups in the community (not excluding some which include persons who are also at the university)

8.4 If my work were to be judged by a "jury of my peers," I would want that jury to be made up most of persons drawn from: (Please number in rank order, with 1 meaning the most preferred jury and 4 the least preferred jury.)

☐ Persons employed at universities in academic and/or administrative capacities

☐ On-campus colleagues and associates

☐ Professional associates (here and elsewhere)

☐ People whom I respect in the community (not excluding some who happen to be at the university)

8.5 It would take some very strong inducements to get me to accept a position at any place other than a university.

strongly agree	agree	undecided	disagree	strongly disagree
☐	☐	☐	☐	☐

8.6 (a) How many books have you published in the last 5 years?

none	1	2+
☐	☐	☐

(b) How many articles have you published in the last 5 years? (Count any papers delivered at professional meetings, but not published, as articles)

none	6-10
☐	☐
1	10+
☐	☐
2-5	
☐	

8.7   (Faculty please ignore this question)
One of my most important responsibilities is to maintain my competence as a university administrator by keeping up to date on educational and educational administrative problems in general, even at the possible cost of neglecting my specific duties at this university.

strongly agree	agree	undecided	disagree	strongly disagree
☐	☐	☐	☐	☐

8.8   Suppose you received a very attractive offer at a university comparable to this one in all major respects, and which would enable you to pursue your professional interests at least as well as you are able at this university. However, the university was located a considerable distance away. How much would each of the following factors weigh in your thinking:

	a great deal	quite a lot	some	hardly any	not at all
having to leave the climate and geographic setting here	☐	☐	☐	☐	☐
having to give up my ties and contacts with people in the community here whose interests are similar to mine	☐	☐	☐	☐	☐
having to give up my friends here	☐	☐	☐	☐	☐
having to give up the recreational opportunities here	☐	☐	☐	☐	☐
having to give up the intellectual atmosphere of the local community	☐	☐	☐	☐	☐
having to close out my financial investments in the area	☐	☐	☐	☐	☐
having to move the family	☐	☐	☐	☐	☐

If this question is completely hypothetical for you, since you would not even consider another offer under any circumstances you can envision at the present time, please check here   ☐

8.9   Control, such as that achieved through rules, regulations, policy statements and the chain of command, should be considered one of the most important activities at this university.

strongly agree ☐   agree ☐   undecided ☐   disagree ☐   strongly disagree ☐

8.10   In my personal opinion, the final word in case of a dispute over something connected with my work should rest with:

☐ (1) my professional colleagues (those in your discipline here, and elsewhere, or, if you are an administrator, then other administrators in positions similar to your own)

☐ (2) the head of my department (or division, or school, or university)

8.11   In matters connected with my work, it is best to develop certain generally agreed upon standards so that each problem is dealt with according to those standards, rather than its own peculiar features.

agree ☐   strongly agree ☐   undecided ☐   disagree ☐   strongly disagree ☐

8.12   In my work, I feel it is important that I limit myself only to my specialized field of competence if I am to do a good job.

strongly agree ☐   agree ☐   undecided ☐   disagree ☐   strongly disagree ☐

8.13   In my work, I feel it is essential that I avoid personally identifying with the person who is seeking my help (student, client, subordinate).

strongly agree ☐   agree ☐   undecided ☐   disagree ☐   strongly disagree ☐

8.14 I believe a person in my position should be given the responsibility he has only if he *demonstrates* his competence, with no consideration at all of whom he happens to be or what his connections are.

strongly agree	agree	undecided	disagree	strongly disagree
☐	☐	☐	☐	☐

8.15 Of how many organizations, clubs, societies, teams or other *voluntary* groups are you a member? (Approximations will do)

Professional or directly work-connected   0 1 2 3 4 5 6 7 8 9 over 9
If you have ever been an officer in any, how many such positions have you filled?   0 1 2 3 4 5 over 5

Social or recreational   0 1 2 3 4 5 6 7 8 9 over 9
If you have ever been an officer in any, how many such positions have you filled?   0 1 2 3 4 5 over 5

Political, community and others   0 1 2 3 4 5 6 7 8 9 over 9
If you have ever been an officer in any, how many such positions have you filled?   0 1 2 3 4 5 over 5

9. LASTLY, ABOUT YOURSELF

9.1 Present age (nearest birthday):

☐ under 25   ☐ 26-30   ☐ 31-35   ☐ 36-40   ☐ 41-45
☐ 46-50   ☐ 51-55   ☐ 56-60   ☐ 61-65   ☐ 66 or over

9.2 Sex: ☐ M   ☐ F

9.3   Number of children: (please circle the correct number) 0, 1, 2, 3, 4, 5, 6 or more.

9.4   Race: ☐ White
                 ☐ Negro
                 ☐ Mongoloid

9.5   Country of birth of father _____

9.6   Father's education:

      Years of schooling completed: ☐ 11 or less.   ☐ 12.   ☐ more than 12.

      Degree(s) obtained if any: _____

      Mother's education:

      Years of schooling completed: ☐ 11 or less.   ☐ 12.   ☐ more than 12.

      Degree(s) obtained if any: _____

9.7   Father's occupation during most of his adult life: (please be specific) _____

9.8   Your place of birth:

      If rural, name nearest city _____

      If urban, name city _____ _____
                                    (state, if U.S.A.)   (country)

9.9   Place in which the greater part of your life up to age 17 was spent:

If rural, name nearest city _____

If urban, name city _____ _____ _____
                                    (state, if U.S.A.)   (country)

9.10 Church affiliation:

☐ Catholic   ☐ None   ☐ Other
☐ Jewish   ☐ Protestant   (If Protestant or Other, please specify _____.)

9.11 Sources of income: (for income tax year 1964)

Percentage of income derived from this source

Academic Salary   _____

Consulting   _____

Income from writing   _____

Other sources (please specify)   _____
                                   100%

9.12 Marital status: (check one)

☐ Single
☐ Married
☐ Divorced, and presently unmarried
☐ Separated
☐ Widowed

If married and male, a question about your wife:

Education of wife's father:

Number of years: ☐ 11 or less
                    ☐ 12
                    ☐ more than 12

Academic degrees, if any: _____

Occupation of wife's father during most of his adult life,
(please be specific): _____

9.13 Your education:

☐ 11 years or less

☐ 12 years

☐ some years of college or university, but no degree received

☐ B.A. (or other bachelor's degree requiring 4 years or more)

If so, what college or university? _____ Year received _____

Field of specialization, if any _____

☐ M.A. or M.S., or other Master's degree requiring at least one year beyond the bachelor's degree.

If so, what university or college? _____ Year received _____

If so, what field of specialization _____

☐ M.D. If so, what university? _____ Year received _____

☐ Ph.D. If so, what university? _____

If so, what field of specialization _____

Year received _____

☐ Other degree than those named.

What degree? _____ What college or university? _____ What field of specialty? _____ Year received _____

9.14 Job history:

Title of present position (if more than one is held, please list the other(s): _____

Department, if any _____ .

List below only positions held for 9 months or longer: (please start with *most recent* position)

Kind of Position	Name of Employer	Period of Employment
1.		
2.		
3.		
4.		
5.		
6.		
7.		
8.		

9.15 This question is optional

Income data will enable us to perform a number of important analyses. We recognize, however, that persons are, understandably, reluctant to reveal what they feel is a personal matter. Would you therefore simply provide an approximation as follows:

Total income from all sources, before taxes, in the 1964 tax year (i.e., an amount no more than 25% above or below your actual income).

$ _____

THE REMAINING QUESTIONS ARE FOR ADMINISTRATORS ONLY

9.16 How do you feel about your administrative job(s) at the university?

☐ (1) excellent. I can ask for nothing better

☐ (2) good.

☐ (3) fair.

☐ (4) poor. I hope to make a change

9.17 Think now of your predecessor in your position. How long did he hold the position? _____ years. How long did the man before him hold the position? _____ years.

9.18 What are your plans for the future so far as your work is concerned?

☐ Continue in my present position, or one much like it

☐ Move up to a higher administrative position, or one like my present one at a more prestigious university, if an opportunity comes up

If so, what would represent the culmination of your ambition in administration? _____

_____

☐ Get into, or return to, teaching or research in this, or another university

☐ Leave university work altogether and go into some other kind of institution

9.19 How would you describe your feelings about your career thus far:

☐ Good progress thus far, and the future looks good

☐ Good progress thus far, but I'm not at all sure about the future

☐ Good progress and I feel reasonably satisfied with where I am. I doubt that anything much better will turn up

☐ My career has had so many ups and downs that I'm not at all sure just what my next move will be or ought to be

☐ I am blocked where I am and will have to move out to get ahead

☐ The future does not look good at all and I do not have any good hope for the long-range future

9.20 Suppose you were leaving the university for another position, and the administration asked you to recommend someone as your replacement. Suppose, further, that you knew your views would weigh heavily in the final decision. What kind of person would you recommend, and what kind would you oppose? Let us assume, further, that you are leaving your present position with great reluctance and that you have great affection for the university. Hence you want to see yourself replaced with the person most likely to do a top-notch job after you have gone. In answering this question, choose one of the alternatives indicated by the initials under each attribute. These initials stand for the following:

am   absolutely must be, or must have

ps   preferably should be, or should have

m   may or may not be, or may or may not have

pn   preferably should not be, or should not have

an   absolutely must not be, or must not have

EXAMPLE:

brown hair	black hair	white hair	red hair
am <u>ps</u> m pn an	am ps <u>m</u> pn an	am ps m <u>pn</u> an	am ps m pn <u>an</u>

In this example, we have underlined the alternatives to indicate the reply of a person who felt that the person who would replace you *preferably should have* brown hair, *may or may not have* black hair, *preferably should not have* white hair, and *absolutely must not have* red hair. Please be sure to check *each* attribute.

church member	liberal in his politics	A Doctor's degree other than or in addition to the Ph.D.
am ps m pn an	am ps m pn an **53**__	am ps m pn an **58**__
48__		
Protestant	Democrat	university experience
am ps m pn an	am ps m pn an **54**__	am ps m pn an **59**__
49__		

Catholic
am ps m pn an **50**___

Jew
am ps m pn an **51**___

conservative in his politics
am ps m pn an **52**___

Republican
am ps m pn an **55**___

Bachelor's degree
am ps m pn an **56**___

Ph.D. degree
am ps m pn an **57**___

research experience
am ps m pn an **60**___

a scholar
am ps m pn an **61**___

personally ambitious
am ps m pn an **62**___

easy going
am ps m pn an **63**___

sold on the importance of pure research
am ps m pn an **64**___

graduate work in an academic discipline
am ps m pn an **65**___

sold on the importance of applied research
am ps m pn an **66**___

graduate work in one of the physical or biological sciences
am ps m pn an **67**___

(if the position is in a professional school)
experience as a practitioner
am ps m pn an **68**___

previous experience in a university administrative position of some sort
am ps m pn an **69**___

graduate work in one of the liberal arts disciplines or social sciences
am ps m pn an **70**___

If there is an attribute other than listed above which you think would be *absolutely essential* or which would *completely disqualify* a person, please mention it (or them, if more than one) below:

absolutely essential _____

completely disqualified if _____

9.21 Assuming other things are equal, which of the following would you recommend as your replacement?

☐ The person more acceptable to outside persons and groups that the university must deal with (legislative, major sources of endowment, etc).

☐ The person more acceptable to the faculty of the university as a whole.

ANNOTATED BIBLIOGRAPHY

The following list includes only those theoretical works in sociology that the writers feel to be most relevant to the issues addressed in the study of university goals. It is not intended, of course, to be comprehensive. It does not include either works written by educational administrators themselves or works that presumably are familiar to educational administrators and to faculty interested in the process of academic administration.

BEN-DAVID, JOSEPH, and ZLOCZOWER, AWRAHAM. "Universities and Academic Systems in Modern Societies." *European Journal of Sociology*, III (1962), 45–84. A good study of factors associated with university "eminence," considered historically and cross-nationally.

BERELSON, BERNARD. *Graduate Education in the United States*. New York: McGraw-Hill Book Co., 1960. A careful examination of the graduate school and its essential place in the university. This book influenced the selection of universities employed in the study.

BLAU, PETER M., and SCOTT, W. RICHARD. *Formal Organizations*. San Francisco: Chandler Publishing Co., 1962. This widely used book has in a very short time become a classic. It represents one of the best theoretical summaries of the sociological literature on organizations.

CAPLOW, THEODORE. *Principles of Organization*. New York: Harcourt, Brace, and World, 1964. A meaningful integration of the more important sociological studies of formal organization. This book influenced the approach to goals employed in the study, with particular reference to the relationship between goals and prestige.

DUFF, SIR JAMES, and BERDAHL, ROBERT O. *University Government in Canada*. Report of a Commission Sponsored by the Canadian Association of University Teachers and the Association of Universities and Colleges of Canada. Toronto: University of Toronto Press, 1966. A valuable comparative study of university government.

ETZIONI, AMITAI. *A Comparative Analysis of Complex Organizations*. New York: Free Press of Glencoe, 1961. In addition to summarizing the sociological literature on organizations, Etzioni seeks to characterize organizations by type of control system.

GOODMAN, LEO A., and KRUSKAL, WILLIAM H. "Measures of Association for Cross Classifications." *Journal of the American Statistical*

164 ANN

A— of the
g
KATZ *Orga-*
n tempt
t from
s
MARC Rand
M bly in
q ences.
P ers by
S ourke,
P
ORLA *ation.*
W ant to
th es on
u
PARS ormal
O *odern*
S state-
m ty (or
o
THOM Graw-
H oward
o ays of
re lucing
u